BRIGHT NOTES

AN INTRODUCTION OF WALLACE STEVENS

Intelligent Education

Nashville, Tennessee

BRIGHT NOTES: An Introduction of Wallace Stevens
www.BrightNotes.com

No part of this publication may be used or reproduced in any manner whatsoever without written permission, except in the case of brief quotations in critical articles and reviews. For permissions, contact Influence Publishers http://www.influencepublishers.com.

ISBN: 978-1-645424-68-0 (Paperback)
ISBN: 978-1-645424-69-7 (eBook)

Published in accordance with the U.S. Copyright Office Orphan Works and Mass Digitization report of the register of copyrights, June 2015.

Originally published by Monarch Press.
Austin Fowler, 1965
2019 Edition published by Influence Publishers.

Interior design by Lapiz Digital Services. Cover Design by Thinkpen Designs.

Printed in the United States of America.

Library of Congress Cataloging-in-Publication Data forthcoming.
Names: Intelligent Education
Title: BRIGHT NOTES: An Introduction of Wallace Stevens
Subject: STU004000 STUDY AIDS / Book Notes

CONTENTS

1) Steven's Life and Work 1

2) Analysis of Selected Poems 13

3) Criticism 78

4) Bibliography 85

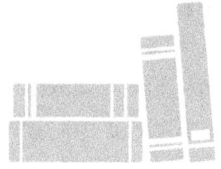

INTRODUCTION TO WALLACE STEVENS

STEVENS' LIFE AND WORK

STEVENS' LIFE AND WORK

Biographical Introduction

In an age when most artists, even poets, felt compelled to market their products as if they were detergents, Wallace Stevens, one of the comparatively few great American poets, chose to let his poems speak for themselves. The result of this lifelong reticence (or, to use a word no longer in fashion, dignity) is that the facts of Stevens' life are meager. This meagerness of biographical detail is a mixed blessing. On the one hand, it keeps the sentimental critic from reading the poems as if they were merely diary entries of the poet's life; on the other, it focuses so much attention on the one unusual (for a poet) fact of Stevens' life, that many forget to look at the poems. That is: Stevens was a very successful businessman. Trained as a lawyer, he chose to go into business and for many years, almost until the end of his long life, was Vice President of the Hartford Accident and Indemnity Company. Persons in the arts community talk as if he were, in some obscure way, a traitor; the members of the business community, who did not know he was a poet at all, have not made their reactions to his dual existence available.

But for Stevens this duality did not exist: he was a fine businessman who was also one of America's artistic geniuses. He may perhaps have hoped that some day America would approach the maturity of outlook which accepts the fact that poetry is as essential to the Nation's welfare as washing machines and the space program, and take it for granted that man has needs beyond the capacity of the local supermarket to fill. He would have agreed with the biblical injunction that 'Where there is no vision the people perish," but he would also have understood that people don't realize the importance of food until their stomachs are empty.

The Facts Of His Life: Wallace Stevens was born in Reading, Pennsylvania, on October 2, 1879. His father was a lawyer. On his mother's side, the Zeller's, Stevens claimed Dutch ancestors, religious refugees who, after living for fifteen or twenty years in the Schoharie region of New York, went down the Susquehanna to Tulpehocken in Pennsylvania. In 1897, he matriculated at Harvard, where he stayed until 1900. After some time spent in New York as a reporter for the *New York Herald Tribune* in the old ornate building which still stands on Park Row, he went to the New York Law School (which up until a few years ago also stood on Park Row) and graduated in 1903. In 1904 he was admitted to the New York Bar and practiced in New York City until 1916. During these years, in which he worked hard to develop a successful law practice, he maintained his relationships with artists and writers in nearby Greenwich Village, among them William Carlos Williams (who was to become a successful doctor and author of the great American epic, Paterson); Marianne Moore (who shares with Emily Dickinson the first rank among American poetesses); and e. e. cummings, whose experiments in breaking up words and patterning his lines upon the page were to identify him in the minds of most Americans as the very model of the advance guard poet.

As far as is known, no manuscript poems survive before 1913, when Stevens was about thirty-four years old. In 1914 he had four poems published in the magazine Poetry. From then on he was a consistent contributor to the little magazines. He published, for instance, in Alfred Kreymborg's periodical Others such famous pieces as "Peter Quince at the Clavier." In 1915 he published what was to become his most celebrated (if not his greatest) poem in Poetry; the first version of "Sunday Morning." In 1916 he published the first of two verse plays, *Three Travelers Watch the Sunrise*, and in 1917 the second, *Carlos Among the Candles*.

In 1916, moving to Hartford, he joined the Hartford Accident and Indemnity Company, of which he became Vice-President in 1934. Up to this time he had, apparently, written comparatively infrequently. Now he began to write and publish prolifically. In 1916-1917, according to Frank Kermode in his book *Wallace Stevens* (see bibliography), he published about a poem a month; in 1918 there were fifteen poems, including the very important "Le Monocle de mon Oncle." By 1923 he had published about a hundred poems. During this time he was attempting, as he said, to perfect "an authentic and fluent speech" for himself.

Publishing History: In 1923, when Knopf published *Harmonium*, Stevens was forty-five years old. In the time-honored fashion for early works of poetry, few copies were sold. For a number of years after this Stevens wrote few poems. A second edition of *Harmonium* was published in 1931. In 1935, he published *Ideas of Order*; in 1936, *Owl's Clover*; in 1937, *The Man with the Blue Guitar & Other Poems*; in 1942, *Parts of a*

World and *Notes toward a Supreme Fiction*; in 1944, *Esthetique du Mal*; in 1947, *Transport to Summer*; in 1950 *The Auroras of Autumn*. In 1954, when he was seventy-five, he published his *Collected Poems*. Besides these there is the collection of his prose essays and lectures, published as *The Necessary Angel* in 1951. In 1957, *Opus Posthumous* was published with an introduction by Samuel French Morse, who is writing an official biography. We must wait for this biography for a fuller disclosure of the facts of Stevens' life.

Stevens' Poetic; Background And Influences

Stevens kept a notebook in which from time to time he jotted down, (as did such earlier American writers as philosopher-poets Emerson and Thoreau) conclusions he had come to about poetry, language, existence. Among these aphorisms, published under the title "Adagia" in *Opus Posthumous*, is the following: "French and English constitute a single language" and "The Americans are not British in sensibility." These statements offer as useful a springboard as any for an analysis of Stevens' poetry.

First of all, they will help explain a number of characteristics of the poet which might otherwise baffle the reader: his exotic and particular vocabulary, his seemingly incomprehensible subject matter, the central notions of his work, the "ideas" he offers.

In addition, they will serve to show the place that Stevens holds in the tradition of Western, especially American, poetry.

French Influences On Stevens: Stevens, like Whitman before him, does not limit himself to the conventional vocabulary of the English language. His poetry is full of French words and phrases.

AN INTRODUCTION OF WALLACE STEVENS

We can say, in a general way, that there are two reasons for this: one is the particular circumstances of time and place in which Stevens began as a poet; another is that they were Stevens' deliberate choice. Let us take these separately. In the latter part of the Nineteenth Century, many English poets, believing that the traditional **conventions** of English poetry were exhausted, sought new forms of expression, new subject matter. The reader may perhaps know of Gerard Manley Hopkins' (1844-1888) attempts to introduce "sprung rhythm" (a return in some measure to Anglo-Saxon and Elizabethan practice) as a poetic device. Since Hopkins' poetry was not published in his own time, it is difficult to say what kind of effect it would have had on the poetry of his contemporaries.

Many English poets, on the other hand, found inspiration in the tradition of French poetry. At first this took the form of imitating French structures only (such as the villanelle, the ballade, the triolet) and we may study the success of these attempts in the poetry of Oscar Wilde and Austin Dobson, to name only two. But the influence began to grow stronger. During the Nineteenth Century the French had undergone a revolution in poetry. Such poets as Baudelaire, Rimbaud, Mallarme, Verlaine, Valery and Laforgue had contributed a number of radical ideas about the nature and function of poetry. It would be difficult to do full justice to these ideas in this limited space. Suffice it to say that among others, these are some of the essential aspects: The poet's duty is to enlarge the real by rejecting those images and forms of expression, those ways of seeing and understanding and feeling, which are no longer valid or "true"; he must get rid of the "garbage" which inevitably collects in a culture; he must re-see, re-feel, re-imagine existence, "purify the language of his tribe," which is full of dead words, and give the world back to the people.

Violence, Decadence, Mystery: How does the poet do this? As Rimbaud suggests, by breaking out of the cage (which the traditional ways of seeing things becomes) by a violent assault on **convention**, by cracking up the language, by violent assaults on one's own senses. Only by doing this can one escape imprisonment and find the real world. Baudelaire suggested new subject matter, giving imaginative form to material conventionally rejected as the subject matter of poetry. For Baudelaire this material was the city, for instance, or disease, or sin, or evil. To get away from the convention, maintained so deadeningly by the industrialized middle class, one had to shock, search out decadent and debased existences. One must in fact, descend into hell before one gets to reality which is heaven. Baudelaire also promulgated the notion of "correspondences," i.e. that a resonance, or reverberation is set up between objects which, dissimilar, when placed together, are seen to have an affinity, to be analagous, to create a third object. This third object is the poem, the real discovery, the new entity. The creative poet sees how one thing is a symbol for another; the poet "finds" symbols.

This idea bore fruit in what is called the "Symbolist Movement." It was of tremendous importance to the whole development of modern poetry. Such poets as Mallarme went even further. He said that the poet must merely provide the symbols; it is the reader's task to discover the meaning of the symbols, which consequently leads to the notion of the poem as a structure or object entirely separate from the poet, having its own mysterious being. It is mysterious, however, only because its meaning is itself. One cannot paraphrase it. What, one might ask is the "meaning" of a cloud, or a rock? But as one does not ask this, neither should one ask the "meaning" of a poem. "A poem should not mean, but be" says the American poet, Archibald Macleish. Among this group, the poems often comprised symbols offered only as images, without any connectives. Stevens was deeply influenced by these ideas of the Symbolists. In his own country, such people as Ezra Pound were already promulgating them as early as the 1990's. Already deeply read in the whole literature of the French - whose orderliness, intelligence, wit and linguistic sensitivity he found congenial to his own talents and personality - Stevens, with others, quickly accepted Pound's imagist dictum that the poet must discard everything from his poetry but images. From his earliest publication until the end, Stevens was never to discard the image and the symbol as basic components of his poetry. Here is an example from an early poem: "The houses are haunted/By white nightgowns." and one from a very late poem: "The owl sits humped. It has a hundred eyes." The value of the image is the value of uncluttered and accurate re-creation; the value of the symbol is the value of analogy. Since the world is complex, an accurate realization of it must be complex, one thing must stand for many. So we attain resonance, reverberation, density.

The British Influence On Stevens: In spite of all that has been said, Stevens is also one of the finest products of the British tradition of English poetry. In his great **blank verse** we hear the descendant of Shakespeare, Milton, and Wordsworth. The student cannot fully appreciate such a masterpiece as "Le Monocle de mon Oncle" unless he can hear the echoes and variations of Shakespeare's **sonnets** that it contains. Without familiarity with the blank-verse tradition of Milton, one cannot begin to savor the majestic cadences of "Sunday Morning." Stevens' sensibility, as he himself suggests, was a compound of the French and English; but in sum total, it was something new - it was American.

The American Influence On Stevens: But no one could mistake Stevens himself for anything but an American. His poems are full of American names - place names, personal names: New Haven, Hartford, Florida, Jersey City - such names abound. His poems are a "marriage of flesh and air," they "occur as they occur": in a local cemetery, on the way to the bus, looking out a hotel window, passing the city dump. And since Stevens never left America, the vast majority of these "occurrences" are specifically localized. It is American speech which is the yeast of his **diction**; American air which pours through his sky. American places which he has realized.

He saw himself as a continuator of that imaginative realization of America started by Emerson, by Walt Whitman. The poet was the expressor and the expression of his place. "The greatest poverty is not to live/In a physical world," that is, one is poor if one lives in fancy or dream. In Emerson he would find a congenial philosopher; for Emerson too, the world was an analogue of a transcending reality. In the specific and particular thing one found a symbolic correspondent for the overreaching, non-sensate world; but it was through the sensate world that one saw the other. For Stevens the world was not real until it was realized through imagination. The poet is he who is able to imagine from the "green" world available to his eyes, ears, touch, smell, the "blue" world which is the real one. People without the ability to transform the sensate world live in "poverty" because in fact they don't "see" the "green" world either: they live in the dead world of the past which, though it may have flourished once, is gone. Stevens said, calling upon the genius of imagination which dwelled in him, "My dame, sing for this person accurate songs." "This person" was, and is, his "tribe," the American people, who, living in the poverty of ancient and decayed visions, need a real world, an accurate world.

Stevens called poetry "the supreme fiction," by which he meant simply that the imagined recreation of the real is not necessarily the real, it is a map which is useful for the time. Each age, each culture must make new maps: the thing "out there" remains; "the plum survives its poems." This does not mean that the map is fanciful, the product of mere dreaming. The poet must get rid of "seem" and by the accuracy of his vision, substitute "be." But always, the world is changing. One looks at old snapshots which were accurate in their time - but the subjects of those pictures are now old or dead. A major poet's maps last longer than others - sometimes forever, if he is accurate enough. Stevens is an "accurate" mapmaker; he is a major poet.

Stevens' Terms

Reality And Imagination: I have used the terms "reality" and "imagination" a number of times in the previous section. Let us now analyze these terms as they are ordinarily used and then as Stevens understood them. Ordinarily, when we use the word "reality" we mean the world that is given to us by our senses - we mean what we see, what we smell, what we touch, what we hear, what we taste. Our assumption is always that everyone else sees, smells, touches, hears and tastes the same things we do. If they don't, there is something wrong with them. What we never stop to realize is that we all share this common reality because it has been organized for us, and from childhood on we are unconsciously trained to adopt a common understanding of what is "out there." If you stop to think for a moment about, say, the way in which an Australian aborigine and an American secretary might see a typewriter or an animal track in the dust you will perceive the importance of training. What makes for this difference of perception, aside from individual mentality, but difference in culture, difference in training? The fact of the matter is that each culture actually perceives a different world.

What brings this difference about? Many things: usefulness (the aborigine does not need a typewriter to survive; the secretary does not need to understand animal tracks to survive - she can go to the local supermarket), or if you want, vision, which is another word for imagination. Most people understand imagination to mean inventiveness or, in a more limited sense, fancifulness. "Boy," you say about someone with a flair for rich embellishments, "what an imagination he has." More precisely, this is what Coleridge called fancy; that is, fancy is combining elements which one hadn't thought of combining before - it is the talent which good chefs or interior decorators have. Imagination is creation: it is the ability to bring something new into existence by the seeing beyond the obvious, by plunging through the patterns which training and culture have fixed. Shakespeare had imagination, Einstein had imagination, Da Vinci had imagination. The test, it would seem, of imagination is this: if this person had never lived, can we say that we would have what he gave us? It is possible to predict for instance, a Dior gown, but not a Hamlet; it is possible to predict the computer, but not Einstein's theory of relativity.

Stevens' Use Of Terms: For Stevens, "reality" is what the senses give us, the basic, fundamental data. However, it is meaningless until it is organized, "realized" by the imagination. Who "realizes" this? The man of imagination; called variously, the "hero," the "primitive," the "good man." By a peculiar talent, he is able to see things "as they are" not as they "seem." The union between the physical thing (a rock, a river, a landscape, a house) and the man of imagination produces a "fiction," that is, something which was not there, something new. The union is a "marriage," and like a marriage, is more than the total of its parts. The poet, by doing this, brings order out of chaos. He invents, or finds a "mundus" (Latin for "world").

A Glossary Of Stevens' Terms

Anecdote: Stevens titles a number of his short poems "anecdotes." Ordinarily an anecdote is a brief account of an event, usually biographical. Originally it meant facts of history not published as yet -as for instance short accounts of famous men not officially part of the historical record. In Stevens, an anecdote is usually a poem which puts together elements of an opposite nature. These opposites are then shown to be resolvable or even identical.

Blank Verse: Unrhymed iambic **pentameter**. Pentameter is a line measure of five (penta) feet. A foot is a measure of stressed and unstressed syllables. Here is an example of an iambic **pentameter** line which you yourself might have spoken: "Today/I walked/across/the park/to school."

Imagists: A group of poets, American for the most part - notably Ezra Pound, Amy Lowell, Hilda Doolittle - who flourished from 1912-1914. They sought to use ordinary language, to use the whole world as subject matter, to present the reader with a sharply perceived detail. They were influenced by the Japanese haiku form (where the final image is a "realization" of the previous, common images) and ordinarily wrote in **free verse** (non-patterned by meter, or syllable stress). Here is Pound's famous example called "In a Station of the Metro (French subway"): "The apparition of these faces in the crowd:/Petals on a wet, black bough."

Symbolism: Many men have believed that the physical concrete world of the senses "stands for" another, non-physical world, a "higher" reality. In other words the visible world is a symbol of the invisible world. The Romantics generally believed this to be true and modern poetry derives from Romanticism.

Thomas Carlyle in Sartor Resartus says that in "the symbol the infinite is made to blend itself with the finite, to stand visible." A private symbol is one not usually accepted (Dali's melting watch.) Stevens has many private symbols. A conventional symbol is one which most people have come to accept for what it is worth (the nightingale as a symbol of loss or nostalgia or melancholy; the rose as a symbol of beauty, perfection, loveliness). But the symbol rightly discovered has great force because it means more than one can ever say it means. Why this is so, no one has ever been able to discover. But it is so.

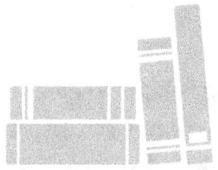

INTRODUCTION TO WALLACE STEVENS

ANALYSIS OF SELECTED POEMS

"Earthy Anecdote"

Introduction: Stevens believed that there are products of the imagination which are not susceptible of rational analysis. These products have their own being as poetry. Here in "Earthy Anecdote," the first poem of *Harmonium*, we have such a product. The "bucks" (which are probably antelopes, but may be Indian "bucks" - improbable - or the "buckboards" of the early settlers) clatter over Oklahoma. Their opponent is the "firecat." What is the reader to make of it? Stevens' persistent interest in America, and especially in what happens to the European mind in America, offers some clue

Summary: In five brief statements Stevens tells his "anecdote" (see glossary above): Whenever the bucks went "clattering" about Oklahoma a firecat was in the way. They swerved right because of it, they swerved left. This happens continuously. Then the firecat closes his eyes and sleeps.

Comment: Opposing forces are set before us - the bucks who wish to run forward freely. There is the firecat, who is (for what reason we are not told, perhaps out of devilment) against this freedom of movement. The bucks are easily swerved aside. It is almost a game which the firecat plays. Later, bored perhaps, he sleeps. On one level - the level of the anecdote itself - this is perfectly meaningful. On another level, assuming the bucks might be symbolic of the early settlers, it suggests how fear of the unknown (the wild, unrealized spirit of the land) frightened them this way and that way. On a third level, the firecat may symbolize any restrictive force in life, which through fear, we allow to direct us from our object.

Form And Style: As is true of a considerable body of Stevens' work, the lyric is written in **free verse**. It has no present pattern of **stanza** length or meter. Each section is a separate sentence. The **diction** is extremely simple; the sentences "statemental."

Question: What is the meaning of "Earthy Anecdotes"?

Answer: Stevens has said the "meaning" of a poem is itself. We can make some paraphrase of it, however. Free wild things, or the free spirits of men, seek to go where they will, but something prevents them. This "something" may in fact not be malevolent at all, but merely the playful nature of things. It is our own fear which throws us off course.

"The Paltry Nude Starts On A Spring Voyage"

Introduction: Botticelli, the great Italian painter, pictured Venus born from the sea on a great shell. In this he followed classic convention. The sea has always been identified as the source of life. Modern science supports this older belief. Venus, as the Goddess of Love, is also the Goddess of regeneration. In spring, the time of regeneration, she starts her voyaging.

Summary: In Stevens, contrary to classic prerequisite, Venus does not start off on a shell, but on a bit of seaweed. She is identified with the wave itself on which she travels. She seeks the deep, the interior of the sea. She is sped by the wind, and, identical with the wave, touches the clouds. But she is young, "paltry"; in high summer, rich and full, she will attain her calm completeness.

Comment: The nude is "paltry" because she is young. It is earliest spring, and she is the impulse of spring. She is also the spirit of the imagination, seeking the deep, the fountain of existence. She returns to the sea. But this, compared to the later exploration is mere play. Then, when the winds and storms of spring have subsided, she will find the deeper meanings of life. Stevens often identified the seasons with his meanings. Spring is (as is traditional) the time of voyaging; for the imagination it is the time of exploration, of first flowering, of youth. Summer is lush and full and the peak of imaginative powers; it symbolizes paradise. Autumn is the time of decay, of weather, of doubt and questioning. Winter is identified with the primeval, the basic, the denuded mind faced with things as they are, the world without imagination.

Form and Style: This beautiful lyric is in **free verse**. The lines move in accurate symmetry to the events described, on the hesitating, onrushing motion of the waves themselves. The reader is directed to think of Venus and the classical tradition by the denial, in the first line, that a shell is used for transportation. This is an American creation, this nude, and like the poet she is not content: she would leave the shore, the harbors and seek the deep. The **diction** is exact but not common. The "high interiors" of the ocean are its depths, conceived as great chambers. "Spick torrent" means glittering torrent.

Question: What is the significance of Stevens' title?

Answer: It is quite exact to what occurs in the poem. The girl, symbolic of regeneration, is nude because this is the classical convention. She is "paltry" because she is young, not full and complete. The poem narrates the beginning of her voyage. It is spring, because spring is synonymous in the poets' usage with that first impulse of the imagination which seeks the primordial deeps of existence.

"The Plot Against The Giant"

Introduction: The giant in Stevens is often a symbol of unorganized reality. Undisciplined and primitive, he can be "plotted against," that is, caught. Here we have three voices (all female) telling how they shall subdue him. There are elements of sexual contest in the poem. The third girl may be identified with the poet's muse, his imagination.

Summary: The first girl, who thinks of him as a "yokel," a country bumpkin, suggests that such civilized odors as that of the geranium will check him. The second girl will appeal to his savage love of color. The third, however, will cause him to bend and listen to her voice as she whispers "heavenly labials in a world of gutturals."

Comment: The giant, chaotic reality can be subdued in various ways, some more successful than others. Of these the sense of smell is least effective, but still the world may be in some measure disciplined and made understandable by symbolic odors and perfumes. But by these reality is merely "checked," or stopped momentarily. Color may also be used. Color here stands for sight. Visual designs, pictures and the like may "abash" reality, the visual arts may cow it. But the way to "undo" "le pauvre" (the poor fellow) is by words; not just any words, but "heavenly labials," the tongue and speech of the poet, for the giant is used only to "gutturals," to the harsh, primitive, common sounds of the language.

Form And Style: Notice the neat division of approaches to reality in this **free verse** poem and how precise Stevens' **diction** is in showing how smell, sight, and speech can symbolize the real. The giant is a private symbol (see glossary above) but easily understood by the reader. Each girl here has character. One might say they are young, charming, sure of their feminine charms. We might almost be listening to a group telling how they shall overcome a campus hero without any particular delicacy of manner. The "heavenly labials in a world of gutturals" might sum up Stevens whole theory of poetry.

Question: Why is there said to be a "plot" against the giant?

Answer: Because reality is too large (a giant) to be taken except by stratagem. One must surprise it if it is to be undone. Of course, the tone here is playful: the young ladies speak in character. The meaning, however, is serious. One way of seeing how the artist works is to listen to young ladies discussing how they will "civilize" a rather large and uncouth adolescent. It is noticeable that the third girl (who will succeed) has pity on and sympathy for this "poor fellow," whereas the others look down upon him or merely wish to confuse him.

"Domination Of Black"

Introduction: Henry Wells in a recent book (see Bibliography) calls this poem one of Stevens' "most lyrical and symbolic works." Stevens submitted it to an anthology called *This Is My Best*. Along with the poem he offered an explanation - of the choice, an explanation which goes far towards clarifying his idea of the nature of poetry. In it he defends the autonomy of poetry as a way of knowing, different in kind from other ways of knowing. "Poetry is poetry," he says, "and one's objective as a poet is to achieve poetry." The poem's importance is in itself, not in any paraphrase. And so at a time when there were those who insisted that the poem must have a political or social objective (the 30s and 40s), Stevens comes out foursquare for the integrity of poetry in itself.

Summary: This poem is organized as a piece of music might be, about a central **theme**: light and darkness. As flames flicker about the room by the fireplace at night, casting light and shadow like flickering leaves, one is reminded - because of the colors of the flames - of peacocks. In the second **stanza**, the poet moves from the immediate surroundings, the physical room flickering with flame, to a consideration of the flames and colors and shadows - considered, imagined, as peacocks. In the third **stanza** the question is asked: Against what do the peacocks cry - the coming darkness, the terrible wind? In the fourth **stanza** the poet looks out of the window and sees that the constellations, like the flames, like the leaves, like the peacocks are also turning, and that the night is coming. This brings fear to him.

Comment: This poem is constructed in a thoroughly symbolic fashion, but it is quite easy to discern the meaning of the interconnected symbols. Sitting at twilight by the wood-burning fire, the poet sees that the colors of the flames and the flickering shadows resemble the colors and movements of the wind-tossed autumn bushes and trees outside the window. Then the poet thinks of the dark mass of the hemlock (traditionally a tree of mourning, death, and disaster); the sequence is logical. This in turn brings to mind the cry of the peacocks. This is appropriate for a number of reasons: the peacocks, in the coloration of their spreading tails, in the movements of these tails displayed to and by the wind, resemble the flames of the fire, the leaves of the fall woods; also the peacock is an imperial bird, a bird symbolic of beauty and value in itself; also the peacock is said to cry (as does the poet) before disaster comes. In a sense then, the peacocks are in the room, and they are crying. Against what is it they cry? The wind, the encroaching night, the black mass of the hemlocks growing larger and darker as night descends? But beyond the flames, the leaves, the peacocks there are the planets themselves, resembling all these in their fanning, spreading, turning motions: against what do the planets cry? The darkness encroaching is the universal darkness of death, of total destruction. This is what makes the poet fear.

This poem, on the surface so lovely in its motions, so delicate and casual in its musical cadences, deals with one of the most profound emotions man experiences - a sense of his own death, the unknown, and the hardly discernible forces of darkness which always - even in the quiet of one's study at night before a cozy fire - surround him.

Form And Style: Stevens had an intense interest in music and musical forms. Many of his poems are organized according to musical patterns. Here, in a series of four variations based on resemblance, the poet moves back and forth, circling up from a simple lyrical level to a most profound statement about the nature of man's existence. The **diction** is extremely simple, the lines short or long depending on the phrasing. Notice the weaving back and forth of the same words, the repetition of whole lines. These devices serve first as a melodic function; they give the poem an almost extempore, hesitating quality, as if the poet were composing before our eyes. Bit by bit he extends his meaning, "turning" himself in larger and larger circles. These devices of repetition also serve to structure the poem, to hold it together.

Question: Name some devices by which Domination of Black is held together.

Answer: I will select two: resemblance and repetition. The flames resemble the autumn leaves, the autumn leaves resemble the tails of the peacocks, the turning of the peacocks in the wind resembles the turning of the constellations in the heavens. In a step-like movement these resemblances bring us from the poet's study to an overreaching view of the whole earth... Another device is repetition; just as one natural entity (peacock tail, flame) resembles others, so here one phrase resembles another, one line resembles another. Just as, for instance, a musical composition is concluded or resolved by returning to its key, so here the last line repeats a line from the first stanza.

"The Snow Man"

Introduction: This poem is one of Stevens' best known, having been anthologized many times. It sums up, in an almost terrifying way, the mental and emotional requirements the poet must have in order not to be led astray by sentimentality or emotion. He must "see life steadily and see it whole," as Arnold said the great Greek tragic poet Sophocles did. He cannot take comfort in illusion. He must be a "snow man."

Summary: To look at winter, one must have the mind of winter. This means not reading into the desolation and coldness signs of human misery. The wind is not sighing or crying as a human being sighs or cries. Having the mind of winter, one beholds "nothing that is not there," but one is also able to see "the nothing that is" there.

> **Comment: In the Nineteenth Century, Romanticism in essence propounded the oneness of man with nature. Nature was benevolent, friendly, maternal. Wordsworth and his followers found in Nature salve for the wounded spirit, regeneration of wasted vitality. If you have read Arnold's "Dover Beach" you will remember that Arnold found this prescription for salvation inadequate. But he went, perhaps, to the other extreme: nature was malevolent and antagonistic to man. Both of these attitudes (reading into natural phenomena human emotions and feelings) Ruskin called "the pathetic fallacy": that nature "suffered" (pathos, from the Greek) with man or shared his joy, he said, is a fallacy of longing. In "The Snow Man" Stevens is making the same point: we must look at what is "out there" without illusion, or delusion. Only then can we begin to "see" life**

wholly. In another poem "Primitive Like an Orb" Stevens says the same thing. The poet must be like an "orb," an eye, simply "seeing" what is out there, restraining his "natural" desire to have the world the way he wants it.

Form And Style: Again the **diction** is simple in the extreme, appropriate to the cold, hard, simple, primitive message of the poem. "Shagged" is, of course, the past participle form of the adjective "shaggy." As is often the case with Stevens, the whole poem is one sentence, the parts held together by adjective clauses and conjunctive ("and") additives.

Question: Why does Stevens call this poem "The Snow Man"?

Answer: The poem is called "The Snow Man" because the observer, the poet, must be like "a snow man," such as children make, to live in the reality of this landscape. The "snow man" is, in a sense, inhuman: being made of snow, he does not falsify the element in which he lives. Because winter often symbolizes for Stevens the rock-bottom of existence, he chooses the "snow man" as his symbol of the poet. But he says in other poems that to understand the tropics, one must be a "tropical" man. In other words, one must become the object before one can understand the object. The poet is the one who is able to submerge himself in "what is."

"Le Monocle De Mon Oncle"

Introduction: This, one of Stevens' greatest poems - and a great American poem - is based on the **convention** of the **sonnet** sequence, although the individual sections are not sonnets. The sonnet runs to fourteen lines: each of Stevens' sections is eleven lines. The **sonnet** is written in iambic **pentameter**, however, as is this poem. The **sonnet** traditionally explored the **theme** of love; here Stevens uses a similar form to explore the theme.

Summary: A man of forty or thereabouts, the "I" of the stanzas, considers the problems of romantic love. How can he sustain in middle age the high intensity of his old ardor which filled him with delight and made the universe delightful? With delicate self-mockery he inspects this topic, turning it this way and that, filing memoranda of his conclusions and reactions. Gradually it becomes apparent that it is not merely love which is the question but the entire notion of reality. The student of love has become a master of the real; he will settle for the available. Only then will the least and commonest element of the observed universe become distinct and known.

Comment: The title gives us a number of clues: the French translates as "My Uncle's Monocle;" this in itself conjures up a picture of a rather effete, or perhaps esthetic type, separated from the world by his cultivated sensibility, a student, an observer, his monocle fixed upon existence, but by that very fact somewhat distanced from the real. The cleverness of the title also tells the reader to take a certain rather playful, rather ironical view of the speaker; this view the speaker himself shares. If we see him as slightly ludicrous, so too does he see himself. The reader should, however, keep in mind that this is a dramatic monologue and that Stevens, even as he analyzes himself, is creating a character. Finally, the reader should recall that Stevens uses a number of devices for characterizing himself - the rabbi (master), giant, hero, comedian, clown - and that some of these masks occur in this poem.

In the first stanza, the speaker quotes himself - rolling out a magnificent parody of the Shakespearean manner. That it is to be taken as parody is clearly shown in the third line with its glittering clutch of double negatives. The lady and he have had, perhaps, an argument. Does he succeed in knocking her or merely himself? No matter. Her image is tossed up out of the sea of thought, and grief - which he has attempted to suppress - follows. In spite of the obvious mockery of the inflated rhetoric of much romantic love poetry, no reader can miss in these lines the voice of a great poet, especially in the beautifully sustained elasticity of the last four lines, which snaps like a whip on "bursts."

In the second stanza the speaker faces up sadly to his condition. It is spring, but for him there can be no illusion of the uprush of life. The birds sing farewell to him; he is over the top and going down the other side. Yet - he upbraids himself - he persists in living in a make-believe world of illusion, despite his realization of the true facts. The sages of old, he now considers, used to devote their time to contemplation. Men of the past devoted their energies to intricate and ingenious arrangements of the visible world, as for instance did the barbers of Bath. It is a way of suppressing desire, of sublimating, of making life bearable. But the image of the lady, natural and without artifice, destroys whatever peace of mind he hoped to gain by emulating this practice.

In stanza four, he considers the paradox that to youth the dream of love - like Eve's apple before it was tasted - is sweet beyond imagining. But once tasted, it is found acrid. This is a lesson which one cannot learn except by experience. The gauge of the intensity of existence is love. Now, for the speaker, life is tedious, measured not by the pulsing evening star but by the dull ticking of the firefly. He can remember when it was different.

In stanza six, he says that when "amorists (lovers) grow bald" whatever they say about love resembles the lectures of exiles; the specifics of experience fade, experience becomes typical and universal and gray. Love is a theme for the person in love alone. There are two ways of considering life: the romantic awaits the arrival of a magnificent woman brought by "The mules that angels ride" from "beyond the sun." This "honey" may or may not come. Meanwhile rough soldiers drink and dice. The "honey" of the real comes and goes at the same time. The realist knows this. One can wait forever for "love" that may never come, for inspiration which may not come. Meanwhile, all about us, the real - which is lovable - goes fleetingly by.

In stanza eight, some insight, which he accepts painfully, comes to him. He and the loved one are now, in fact, the fruit of love. Autumnal skies shall observe them rotting in winter rains. This is real at least; illusion is washed away.... This insight, deadly as it is, inspires the speaker. He calls all to witness the "faith of forty." Where can he find sufficient courage to sing a hymn proper to his new creed?... Fops, he continues, living in illusion, water their own "gritty soils" with the gushings of their fancy. A "yeoman," a real man, is sustained by the real, not by fancy. He has the courage to accept the truth of existence. Imagination fructifies existence even as existence remains.

In stanza eleven, he applies his new insight to the question. Consider this, he says, that at the basis of all is sex, though sex is not all. The laughter, the weeping, the heroics, the pain and rhetoric and noble gestures are triggered, nevertheless, by sex. Only last night, while he and his love trembled in romantic anguish by the moon-flooded pool, a frog "Boomed from his very belly odious chords." There you have it, right under your romantic nose.

In twelve, the last stanza, the narrator summarizes. The blue pigeon which he had been watching circle the blue sky, upon fluttering to the ground turns out to be white. He, like a "dark rabbi," when young, observed the whole world from a distance. Now, older, he has a different point of view. Things are not fixed. What one sees depends on what one is, where one is. What is true of the pigeon is true of love, of life, of everything. One must look with love at what is in fact there.

Form And Style: The form, as has been pointed out, is a variant of the **sonnet** cycle or sequence, with certain changes. First of all the true sonnet contains 14 iambic **pentameter** lines rhymed according to certain fixed patterns. Here the stanzas, or sections, contain eleven iambic pentameter lines rhymed variously: sometimes in **couplet** form ("again" - "then," "well" - "syllable"), sometimes in quatrain form (abab), sometimes not at all. Stevens, a master of English rhythm, offers us a tour-de-force of elegant variation. He expects us to note the pompous and overextended rhetoric of the first four lines, to hear the echo in the second section of Shakespeare's famous **sonnet** LXXIII ("That time of year thou mayest in me behold/ When yellow leaves, or none, or few, do hang/ Upon those boughs which shake against the cold,/ Bare ruin'd choirs where late the sweet birds sang."). The second point to note is that this is a **dramatic monologue**. It is, presumably, not the poet who speaks in his own person, but a character created for the part. Browning is given credit for inventing this use of verse; many modern poets (Pound, Eliot, Frost) have developed it to their own purposes. Here Stevens shows us, by tone of voice, by **diction**, by phrasing and by attitude, the personality of the speaker: he is intelligent, cultured, a bit of an amateur, a bit of a philosopher, wise enough to protect himself from laughter by **irony**, but still serious enough in his intention. Forty, balding, not especially energetic, an observer of life rather than an actor, the "lines" of his character emerge as he speaks. It is not Stevens per se: let us say it is a projection of Stevens, Stevens in a costume acting out a part, the real Stevens playfully observing the slightly ridiculous version of himself from the wings. The point of a true dramatic monologue is to develop the psychology of an individual in relation to a particular situation, usually one of stress. Stevens here actually uses "Oncle's" meditation on love to make a profound point about his own notions of reality and the imagination: that the real must be accepted for what it is, not what it seems to be; that imagination re-creates and realizes the universe, but the universe remains as it is.

The language of "Le Monocle de mon Oncle" is, for the most part, ordinary and simple. Some words will not be commonly a part of the student's vocabulary. However, Stevens always uses the perfect word in the appropriate place. "Coiffure" is a headdress; Bath is the famous health resort and watering place in England especially popular during the 18th and early 19th centuries and a gathering place for the dandies (followers of Beau Brummell); "connaissance" is French for knowledge, here meaning total knowledge; "ephemeral" means of brief existence; "amours" mean love affairs; an "amorist" is a lover: The reader will find that the precise meaning of some of Stevens' less common words will give him that delight of exactness which Stevens constantly provides.

Question: Why does the speaker refer to himself as a "dark rabbi" and "rose rabbi" in section XII?

Answer: The rabbi, "master," is also and always a student. He observes and comments and codifies. A "dark" rabbi here means one who looks from a distance, immersed in "lordly study." He does not feel the pulse and motion of existence, hence makes mistakes about its meaning. The "rose" rabbi, on the contrary, is deeply involved in life, is full of compassionate love for its least manifestations, hence makes fewer mistakes about its meaning.

"Metaphors Of A Magnifico"

Introduction: The Imagists, the reader will recall, insisted that narrative and expository transition should be excluded from poetry, and that the poem must be made up of images presented so clearly that the reader should get delight primarily from them alone. Here Stevens, almost playfully, explores the difficulty of capturing the right image, finding a **metaphor** for the elusive insight.

Summary: In **free verse**, the picture is presented: twenty men cross a bridge into a village. What are they, as they present themselves to the mind: twenty men crossing one bridge or twenty bridges, or perhaps one man crossing one bridge? The meaning will not declare itself. The poet begins again. But the meaning will not come, though the poet is certain it is there. He starts again, and again; the voice fades off into silence.

Comment: This poem, as do a number of Stevens', has the tone of the extempore: the reader has almost the impression that he hears the poet composing, moving forward, hesitating, sweeping back to pick up the thread, moving forward again, trying to bring the poem to completion. And yet it is the very sense of incompletion that the poet is striving for. He asks, in a sense, what lies behind the image presented to him? The image has implications of disaster, times of unrest. In the last analysis, the reader will continue the poem. His mind will supply the meaning. Note here how Stevens puts opposites to clashing. Perhaps we may call this a form of "anecdote."

"Ploughing On Sunday"

Introduction: Like the former, this too is a series of images, mixed with strident imitative noises. It is a bold, positive, assertive poem, full of the swirl and movement of wind and light and air. The poet, suffused with creative joy, verbally kicks his heels in the air.

Summary: In a series of five **stanzas** of four brief lines apiece, the poet makes brief assertive statements about the state of the weather, exterior and interior. It is a day on which the wind blows and blusters in the sunlight, the barnyard fowl display their tails to the wind. He calls to Remus to blow his horn, for he, the poet, is ploughing on Sunday, "ploughing North America."

Comment: The verse is full of rustle and light, swift and almost brash in its statements of power. First of all, one ought not to plow on Sunday, but for the poet, the spirit comes when it comes. He will not be restrained by rules. "Remus" recalls to our mind the Uncle Remus of the Joel Chandler Harris stories, the line "blow your horn" recalls the nursery rhyme "Little Boy Blue." Stevens asserts that all North America is his work field. Like Whitman - with whom he here deliberately allies himself in his self-confidence and primitive strength - he takes a whole continent as his subject, his reality.

"Another Weeping Woman"

Introduction: Stevens has sometimes been thought of as being so much the poet of place, of states of mind, and of the workings of the creative imagination that he left no room for statements of ordinary human emotion. This poem of profound grief stands contrary to this impression. We do not know the specific occasion of which the poem treats, but a woman has been deprived by death of a loved one; a husband, a father, a son, a lover. The presentation is so chaste and cautious that it reminds us of those steles on Greek graves commemorating the loss of a loved one.

Summary: The poet suggests to the woman that she pour "the unhappiness out" from her "too bitter heart," for grief will not "sweeten." Only poison can grow in such dark and stagnant waters: "black blooms" of poisonous growth. Imagination, "the cause of being," "the one reality" in this "imagined world," leaves the woman and all that remains is the dead weight of the dead, which fancy cannot quicken or fructify. Because of this the woman "is pierced by death."

> **Comment: The title is meant to remind the reader of those pictures of the weeping woman of Jerusalem, and the weeping woman beneath the cross of the crucified Christ. The last line reinforces this resemblance. Mary, the mother of Jesus, was told that at her son's death "a sword would pierce her heart." So "another" weeping woman is brought into line with the great tradition, given the immortal dignity which the tradition bestows. The statement the poem makes is the stoical statement of the realist, "Let the dead bury the dead."**

Form And Style: These three last short lyrics give some small idea of Stevens' range as a technician. In the first, the note of bewilderment and portentousness is struck by the hesitating rhythms and suggestive images; in the second, simple, primitive joy is announced in a series of tidy images, by brief assertive statements, by the nursery rhythms and references; in the third, a tone of classic dignity, suitable to the great **theme** of grief for a departed one, is caught by the long, slow cadence of the lines, the references to a noble tradition, by the stoic **realism** of the statement.

> "Anecdote Of Men By The Thousand" And "Floral Decorations For Bananas"

Introduction: In these poems, Stevens considers explicitly the relationship he insisted held between man and his environment. Any people's reality is, he believed, an expression of that people's environment. This idea is developed in an earlier long poem, "The Comedian as the Letter C." There he considers two propositions: First, that man is the "intelligence of his soil"; second, that "his soil is man's intelligence." The first proposition is one which is commonly held, that man imposes his idea of the real on his environment, that he is in charge, so to speak, of what is there. Stevens rejects this conclusion, and offers as evidence how the traveller's notions of existence change as he moves, say, from Europe to the tropics, from the tropics to America. No, says Stevens, there is a subtle, a radical alliance between a people and the environment that people dwell in; the reality of that people is the visible expression of the "soil" itself. "The Comedian as the Letter C" is a record of this discovery, a declaration of independence from European reality, a demand for a "real" America. The two poems we will now consider are more explicit considerations of this assumption.

Summaries: "Anecdote of Men by the Thousand" is a series of statements or apothegms, all making the same point: "the soul...is composed of the external world." Hence men are "the intelligence of their soil." This is true all over the world, in every circumstance. So it is that the dress of the women of Lhassa (in Tibet) is "an invisible element" of Lhassa made "visible." The thought is explicit and clear.

"Floral Decoration for Bananas," makes the same point, but the tone is lighter, even gay. The speaker mildly upbraids a friend, whom he ironically calls "nuncle" (a Shakespearean term which primarily means "uncle" but it often used to imply "simpleton" or "dolt") for setting a floral arrangement with bananas for an occasion which makes them totally inappropriate. It is to be a rather formal gathering - restrained, cultured, Eighteenth Century, the women in evening gowns. Here there should be plums in an "18th century dish." With bananas, the women should be bangled and have slanted eyes for bananas are barbarous.

> Comment: In both poems - different in tone, setting, diction and imagery - the same point is made: that there is a relationship between men and their environment. In the first, the tone is oracular, philosophic and direct; in the second, the tone is gay, spritely, odd and clever. So with the vocabulary. In the first the diction is simple, explicit, non-imagistic; in the second the words are densely metaphoric, full of appeals to the senses. In the first the appeal is directly to the intelligence; there is no setting. In the second the appeal is to the reader's imagination: the setting is an ornate room just before a gathering. The first is free verse, the second stanzaic, with a fairly consistent iambic trimeter pattern and consistent rhyme scheme (note that each stanza is seven lines, none rhymed except the fifth and sixth).

"A High-Toned Old Christian Woman"

Introduction: This is another frequently anthologized poem of Stevens. As with the majority of this poet's work, there is no record available of the circumstances which prompted its creation. The title gives us the best clue: the poem is a hard-knuckled refutation of a certain kind of religious stance - let us say rigid, narrow, super-orthodox, unyielding, positive, fanatical - held by the personage of the title. Against this kind of religious attitude the poet speaks, precisely, rapidly, ironically, equally positive in his stance, taking on his antagonist without tenderness but, at the same time, with full awareness of her toughness and respect for her intelligence.

Summary: In this monologue, the speaker (presumably the poet) makes a flat assertion that poetry is "the supreme fiction." That is, it is a construct of the human mind. He goes on to imply that the religious convictions of the old lady are also "fictions," leading her to this agreement "in principle" by a series of logical "proofs." It may be, he ends, that her ascetic and self-denying "heaven" is about equally valid with the joyous projection he imagines and that all her practices are just as valid (or invalid) as his own. This fact will make widows (all those who have lost their loves - see "Another Weeping Woman") "wince." The truth, "fictive things," however, "wink as they will." As a matter of fact, and paradoxically, the "real" seems to take pleasure in making those living in illusion (widows) "wince," especially at the truth.

Comment: Stevens' voice here is dramatic and forceful and argumentative. The speaker pushes his thesis without letup from first statement to last with a brilliant and paradoxical set of propositions, which may leave the reader confused on first reading. A character is created to deliver the ultimatum - for such it is. He is not the quizzical, rather uncertain dandy of "Le Monocle de Mon Oncle" but a fairly powerful and direct personage who is fed up with a particular brand of nonsense and is going to deliver himself of his pent-up conclusion without interruption. Still, the reader is led by the very directness of his assertion to at least one of two conclusions that the "high-toned" old lady's "fictions" are at least as valid as the poet's; that Stevens did not believe in the validity of any religious system beyond its "fictive" value.

Form And Style: In form, "A High-Toned Old Christian Woman" is blank verse throughout, riding on a basic rhythm of iambic

pentameter but full of variants which do much to contribute to the dramatic quality of the poem. Some of the lines are end-stopped (that is, the rhythm and the sentence are completed at the end of the line, as for example in the first line and the fifth), others enjambed (that is, the sense runs over into the next line, overflowing the basic line meter, as for example lines three-four, lines six-seven, and many others). The whole poem is constructed in the form of an argument: the first line is the proposition or thesis, the rest of the statements a demonstration of the validity of the thesis. This tone of dry intellectuality is supported by the sub-points and minor conclusions ("Thus" - "Thus" - "Allow"). But clashing with this is a vigorous imagistic current which rises to a crescendo in lines nineteen-twenty. In lines twenty-one and twenty-two, the poet in effect assumes that this crescendo has vanquished his opponent, and he is free to tweak her nose with some quick verbal snaps. The style, in spite of its **parody** of the academic rhetorician, is basically imagistic. There is a systematic analogy to the building of a church in these images: "Nave" is the middle part of the body of a church; "peristyle" is a row of columns supporting a roof; "flagellants" are ascetics who whip, or flagellate, themselves in punishment for sins.

Question 1: What literary form is "A High-Toned Old Christian Woman" written in?

Answer: It is written in the form of a dramatic monologue.

Question 2: What point does the speaker make in the poem?

Answer: The speaker says that the heaven of the stern old lady is as much a construction of her imagination as poetry is of his. She has, therefore, no right to take that "high-tone" with him as if she were right about existence and everyone else were wrong.

Question 3: What does the poet mean by a "fiction"?

Answer: He does not mean a falsehood, or a lie, or a mere exercise of fancy. "Fiction" here (and throughout Stevens' work) means the highest exercise of the imagination by which existence is "realized," made real. A "fictive thing" is a product of the imagination. Later Stevens was to publish a long poem which investigated the nature of poetry and the poetic imagination, calling it *Notes Toward a Supreme Fiction*.

"The Emperor Of Ice Cream" And "Disillusionment Of Ten O'Clock"

Introduction: Both of these short poems, like the one just treated, are famous anthology pieces. "Disillusionment" is possibly the most famous example of the American **Imagism** School. Perhaps it will make clearer than any other of Stevens' poems how his particular poetry works.

Summary: "The Emperor of Ice Cream": Someone, a woman, has died, and this is the announcement of her death. The two verses are full of directives on how the world is to celebrate it. But the main point is that death is the end of illusion, of "seeming," and in the last analysis there is no other "emperor" but the supreme controller - death himself - here in his downgraded, but nevertheless powerful embodiment as the "Emperor of Ice Cream."

Comment: on "The Emperor of Ice Cream": Death has been "realized" in any number of ways: as a svelte thief, as a corrupted skeleton, as a shadow-hooded figure, even as a kindly physician; why not then as a cigar chewing, fat, tough ice cream vendor, an

impresario of childish pleasures? And why ice cream? - Because ice cream is a feature of celebration. What have we to celebrate: the end of "seeming." One is dead. That is the end. Obtruding into the scene is the actual corpse itself: "her horny feet" leave nothing to have illusions about. Face - says the poet in a double fanfare, one at the end of each stanza - the fact: Death insists on the destruction of all illusion, no matter how the mind conceives it.

Summary: "Disillusionment of Ten O'Clock: The world is dull, it is late evening, the people are going to sleep. Their night apparel shows no imagination: all plain white. Nor are their dreaming minds going to release suppressed but vigorous fantasies. No, even their subconscious minds are blank. Only a drunken old sailor in his boots dreams of exciting adventures.

Comment: on "Disillusionment of Ten O'Clock": The poet practices here a radical synecdoche (giving the part for the whole throughout). The nightgowns stand for the inhabitants who are seen only as their nightgowns; they are erased from reality. They have, in effect ceased to exist except as nightgowns; the gowns flit through the houses like ghosts. The very Puritan blankness of the gowns symbolizes the blankness of the people's minds; they have no imagination. They are going to sleep, and even in sleep they will be dull and blank. In contrast to them there is a visible old sailor, who has a body because his imagination is alive. He dreams of catching tigers in "red weather." Red, in connotation, is the opposite of white. White of course here symbolizes blankness, an unsullied existence without imaginative experiences. "Red" symbolizes life, real existence. The old sailor, in his

"boots" has lived. The whole poem serves as Stevens' indictment of contemporary America: its boredom, its blankness, its acceptance of the poverty-striken life without imagination's vitality. It is a cry for richness and blood in a land where poetry is regarded as unimportant to existence.

Form And Style: "The Emperor of Ice-Cream" is, in form, made up of two eight-line stanzas, unrhymed except in the final two lines of each, and in **couplets** in the final four lines of the second **stanza**. The student will note the repetition of the important last line, its importance strengthened by the isolated rhymes. It is basically a song pattern, but here Stevens gives the verse the power of a public announcement because none of the lines are declarative statements except the doubly affirmed last line; all the rest are imperatives and orders. In style, the verse gets much from Shakespeare, especially in the vocabulary of the fourth line ("wenches dawdle in such dress") and the seventh lines of each verse (which recall Shakespeare's "The Phoenix and the Turtle"). Note to the thick crowding of alliterated "c's" in the third line.

The form of "Disillusionment" is **free verse**. The movement of the lines is "wavy," imitating in form and rhythm the slowly trembling movement of the nightgowns. In style the poem is thoroughly imagistic, giving the reader the images themselves to consider. Spare in these images, the poet yet manages to suggest the rich profusion of possibilities available ("baboons and periwinkles"). Note too that it is not "at Ten O'Clock," which would imply that the speaker was disillusioned, it is "of Ten O'Clock" which implies that the state is inherent in the situation itself.

"Sunday Morning"

Introduction: All critics are agreed that "Sunday Morning" is one of the landmarks of American poetry; Yvor Winters (see Bibliography), a not especially partisan critic, calls it one of the great poems of meditation in English. If we wish to place it in a tradition, we might set it in line with John Donne's *Anniversary poems*, Wordsworth's *Prelude* and *Tintern Abbey*, and certain of the poems of T. S. Eliot, such as *Four Quartets* and "Ash Wednesday." But in the last analysis it is unique, for the profundity of the problem it explores, the richness of its **diction**, the majestic cadences of its rhythms, the fertility of its **imagery** are rarely found combined anywhere else in English outside of Milton and Shakespeare. Its eight sections of fifteen lines each, together form one of the high peaks of English verse. Here Stevens explores the whole question of religion as it relates to reality, the problem of faith in the world - especially in the modern world - and offers his own conclusion.

Summary: The scene is set. It is Sunday morning, but the lady through whose awareness the question of religious faith is to be filtered, is not at church. Instead she sits in her dressing room, a rather ornate affair, lolling in a negligee, over coffee and oranges. It is a sunny morning. Her pet cockatoo is out of its cage and flies about the room. All this helps to put aside but ultimately does not destroy the religious significance of the day, for to all Christians, the day is one on which the death of Christ for the salvation of mankind is recalled: attending church is a declaration of one's belief in the sacrifice, in Christ. The believing Christian orders his life by this belief, but this lady has given up her practice. But as she dreams the "old **catastrophe**" encroaches and troubles the calmness of the day, of her life. In imagination she crosses the seas to Palestine, site of the life and death of Christ.

In section two, having established his **theme** and the subject of his meditation, the poet continues. If Christ is dead to her, why should she give allegiance to the dead? Can't she find in the world itself (in this fruit upon the table, in the beauties of nature) objects of delight and comfort as good as heaven? Wasn't the divine to be found in one's self? Wasn't physical existence the measure and limit of one's total being?

In section three, the poet pursues this thought; the ancients had Jove, whom they imagined, and who filled their lives with meaning. Then, the sky was heaven and also filled with meaning. Are we to fail of imagination sufficient to fill the sky with heaven? Is earth to be the only "paradise" we know? If that is so, the sky - and hence the world - was much "friendlier then than now." Then it was involved in man's life, both in sorrow and joy; now it is only "indifferent."

In section four, the lady speaks. There are moments, she says, as when in early morning the birds sing in their flight over misty fields. But this joy is momentary: "where then, is paradise?" But the poet, beginning to take an active part in the dialogue, says there is nothing that the products of the classic imagination offered which can match the incredibly beautiful offerings of the earth itself.

In section five, the lady counters. She demands "imperishable bliss," a bliss that will endure beyond the moment. The poet answers that that is not to be, for it is the very transitoriness of existence, the imminence of death, which thrills us with the beauty of existence. Without the knowledge that all things are to be obliterated, man would not see the beauty of life. It is the very fact of perishability which makes life wonderful, but this in itself denies "imperishable bliss."

In section six, the poet considers conditions in an "imperishable" paradise. "Does ripe fruit never fall?" There everything is as it is here, but static, still, unchanging. No, it cannot be, for death is the precondition for the knowledge of beauty.

In section seven, the poet offers a tableau, a picture of how the rite of the religion of the earth should be carried out. Men dance and hymn the existence of themselves under and in unison with the sun, source of light, source of life, but without deifying the sun, nor expecting a life for themselves beyond this one. Part of the earth, they accept joyfully the fact of their life as well as the fact of their death.

In section eight, the final section, the poet returns to the lady who now hears a voice which tells her that the tomb of Christ is merely the tomb of Christ, nothing else. Then the poet sums up. We live on earth and are of the earth; about us earth offers its majesty and beauty and power. It is pigeons who, at evening, slide from the sky, not angels or gods, and day ends as life ends, in darkness.

Comment: The position at which the poet in his exploration of the problem of belief arrives is one that is thoroughly agnostic. Any other interpretation of what the poem clearly states cannot be defended. This agnosticism is consistent in Stevens' work. It was seen, for instance, that in "A High-Toned Old Christian Woman," the poet equates the religious doctrines of immortality and paradise with products of the poetic imagination. Stevens is logical according to his own basic premise. Following one offshoot of the Romantic assumption that truth is interior, Stevens arrives at the conclusion that man makes the

"real." The "real" is what he projects onto the visible; it is man himself who makes the visible orderly and understandable to himself. What he says in effect is that people and cultures forget this essential truth of being and begin to give objective and substantial reality to what are, in fact, "fictive things."

Abrams, in his important book *The Mirror and the Lamp* (see Bibliography), offers this distinction between the classic and the romantic modes of knowledge: the classicist believes that reality is "given," it is "out there," and the artist's duty is to hold (as Shakespeare says in Hamlet) the mirror up to nature so that man can see himself and his works undistorted; the romantic, on the contrary, holds that nature is relative and neutral, it is a kind of murky half dark in which the artist, like a lamp, sheds light and gives direction. By this set of definitions, Stevens is clearly Romantic; he is in fact one of the few poets who has devoted his talents to a systematic development of this assumption. It is why, from time to time, his tone becomes didactic, his lines become "statemental"; he often becomes the philosopher of Romanticism, teaching his audience how to see reality. Many of his poems can be seen as demonstration pieces, or models of "how to understand the real," or, more precisely, what approach to take to the visible to see one's relationship to it.

Form And Style: Basically, the poem is a series of personal meditations. It has dramatic content, however, because the poet establishes, in the person of the lady, an opponent against whose position he sets his own. The meter is fairly regular iambic

pentameter. It is of course **blank verse** of the Shakespearean and especially Wordsworth tradition. Its **diction** is remarkably simple. Its great strength as a poem is to be found in what can only be called the orchestration of the rhythms; locked in the basic structure of iambic meter the lines slide and collide and surge with a vitality and complexity rarely matched in American poetry. Here the poet shows himself the absolute master of **blank verse**; he can make it do whatever he wishes. He can paint, rapidly and calmly, the opening scene of indolence and summer Sunday peace, while almost immediately suggesting that this surface of an all but liquid stillness hides turbulence and unrest. He can rise to the two grand statements of natural delight in parts IV and VIII with deceptive ease. To hear these rhythms, the reader should read the poem over and over, as he might listen to a piece of complex music again and again before its importance is laid open to him.

The images here are particularly noteworthy; for instance, the cockatoo of the first section is an alien bird; its presence in the lady's room suggests her dependence on an alien reality. In part IV, the swallow, a native bird, is offered as a symbol of the real. This note is re-emphasized in section VIII with the appearance of the earthy pigeons scattering down in the last sunlight.

Question 1: What is Stevens saying in "Sunday Morning"?

Answer: Stevens holds here that those who believe in creeds not derived from an immediate perception of the visible world are living in illusion, and this illusion can make them unhappy. He is criticizing in particular the brand of Christianity (American, Puritan, New England) with whose practitioners he was most familiar, but he offers his analysis as holding, apparently, for all forms of religion, all forms of "illusion" based on what is not visible. He goes on to say that death is an absolute of human existence, that the knowledge that death ends all without reprieve stimulates the awareness of beauty. Finally he says that men should throw off illusion, accept the conditions of human existence in his terms, and this acceptance will free them to love the world of the sun. Hence they will be happy.

Question 2: Who is the lady of Stevens' poem?

Answer: On one level, the lady is to be taken as a person: that is, she has her own identity. Her setting suggests some of her characteristics: she is well-off, almost pampered, with a sensuous streak; certainly not old, but past her first youth. Her absence from Sunday observance suggests that she has drifted away from the religious tradition in which she was born. She has not, however, shaken the hold the doctrines of that tradition still have on her. On this reading, the poet becomes her teacher, in effect, showing her her errors and indicating how she can overcome them. On another level, she is representative of all who live in such forms of perception.

From another point of view, or on another level of interpretation, the lady may be understood to be an aspect of the poet's own nature, that part which still holds allegiance to illusionary perception. In the poetry of meditation, it is often a formal device for the poet to objectify two aspects of his personality. For instance, in some of W. B. Yeats' poems of meditation, two voices debate some proposition; both voices are projections of the poet himself. This reading of the poem would suggest that Stevens felt the need to express his own inner arguments about the validity of his position.

"Bantams In Pine-Woods"

Introduction: This short lyric is quite often reprinted, usually to demonstrate Stevens' verbal wit and linguistic inventiveness. This aspect of the poet is shown especially in the clever repetition of "an" five times, and the crowd of "h's" leading to the abrupt "halt!" at the termination of the second line. But the poem has more importance than its verbal gymnastics.

Summary: The poet imagines a meeting of wood fowl in the pine forest of America. One huge old bird, with the characteristic strut and self-regard bantams show, is challenged by another. "Who do you think you are?" he says, in effect. "You think the sun itself rises and sets for you. I'm just as important. Get out of the way. You're big now and I'm small, but I'm taking over. I'm not afraid of you."

Comment: If the reader sees that "Chieftain Iffucan of Azcan" is symbolic of the Calvinistic religion, the rest of the poem's meanings fall easily into place. Stevens is reiterating one of his essential points. Calvin's "reality" is only one kind. He is offering another kind. Nor is he going to be frightened off by fear of the "universal cock" who struts about in charge. Let Calvin beware. Stevens' view of reality is going to take over the reality of America. The poem is about the clash in interpretations of reality and the need for America to re-image itself in its own terms. By imagining the contestants (himself as one) in this ontological contest as small wood fowl, Stevens reduces their contributions accordingly. The world is vast, reality is vast. The Calvinist "cock" is large, but he is only "a ten-foot poet among inchlings."

Measured against the total landscape, ten feet is not very big at all.

Form And Style: The poem is constructed of five two-line verses full of spondees (two syllables stressed equally), unrhymed. It is strident and assertive in the extreme. One can almost see the little bantam swollen with rage at the appearance of the larger bird. He descends even to name calling, using infantile invective: "Fat! Fat! Fat! Fat!" Although the poem makes a serious point, it is offered in humorous terms.

"Anecdote Of The Jar"

Introduction: Here again we have a much anthologized verse. It is concerned again with the relationship of man to his environment, specifically the relationship between the products of man and their influence on the environment.

Summary: The poet says that he has "placed a jar" in the wilderness of Tennessee. The first effect of this is that the wilderness became orderly, hence understandable; it "surrounds" the hill where the jar is placed. The second effect is that the wilderness ceased to be "wild." In the midst of it, the jar stands, still having the air of domination. The third effect is that the jar took "dominion" over the landscape. But the jar was "gray and bare," nonproductive, "Like nothing else in Tennessee."

Comment: Most commentators on this poem read it this way: the products of man, specifically artistic products (like the jar, absolutely symmetrical and perfect) make the disorder of the visible meaningful by their influence. The artist reduces the chaos of existence to understandable patterns, and this is, of

course, good. Only one commentator has pointed out that in the last stanza Stevens is apparently denying that this effect is a good one; after all, the jar is "gray and bare" while the rest of "Tennessee" flourishes. But the point that Stevens makes is that any codification of reality is transient, temporary. A "fictive thing" such as the jar (any work of the imagination) has three stages of existence; first, it creates order in chaos; second, chaotic reality, under its influence, systematizes itself; third, it takes "dominion," but it is no longer viable: being "perfect," it is dead. But reality continues, even though "dominated," to produce, to change, to flourish. The student should at this point re-read section VI of "Sunday Morning," where Stevens' position on this subject is more fully given. The jar is a work of art, as is the Calvinist heaven, the lady's "Paradise." But the end effect of a work of art is that it no longer relates to the real, is alien to it. Reality must constantly be reimagined. The marriage of "flesh and air" must continuously be celebrated.

"Life Is Motion"

Introduction: It is to our purpose to look now at this extremely short poem for what insight it gives to Stevens' poetic artistry as analyzed in the preceding page.

Summary: The poet simply offers us a picture and comment. In rural Oklahoma two girls, Bonnie and Josie, dance exuberantly about a stump. They cry out in joy. They are "celebrating the marriage of flesh and air."

Comment: The impulse of mankind is to reduce existence to orderly abstractions, but existence itself is not abstract. Life is not the stillness of Keats' *Grecian Urn* (or the jar of Tennessee) but the pulsing, flowing stream of chaos itself, of which man is a part. Stevens often expresses this notion of "real" existence by means of the dance. Compare for instance his suggestions for the ritual celebration of human existence given to us in section VII of "Sunday Morning."

"To The One Of Fictive Music"

Introduction: In classic times poetic ability was imputed to be the gift of the gods. It was not the individual himself who was responsible for his peculiar and rare talent; it was a gift. Directing poetic inspiration was the muse. Homer, Virgil, Milton, all call upon the muse to aid them in the carrying out of their tasks. Here Stevens too calls upon that power in him (and at the same time conceived of as beyond himself) by which he creates poetry. He calls her "the one of fictive music"; she is the power of the highest reaches of the imagination.

Summary: In a verse more solemn and sustained in rhythm than perhaps any other Stevens wrote, he calls upon the muse, naming her with honorific titles as "queen," "mother," "sister." It is she who weaves the most nourishing, understandable, life-sustaining patterns, although others are also capable of doing so. These other "realizers" of human existence makes earth a "simulacrum" of man's desires, a "gross effigy." She alone gives "motion of perfection." But man has forgotten the great and dreadful muse of the imagination - to his sorrow. Now the poet calls upon her. "Unreal," (because first she is "unrealized," and second does not exist except as a power) "give back to us what once you gave:/The imagination that we spurned and crave."

> **Comment: Stevens seems to be doing here what his philosophic position stands against; that is, he apparently gives objective reality to a force or power outside himself. Whether he saves himself from an awkward logical stance is perhaps moot. In any case, the verse is majestic, a powerful evocation, an orotund hymn full of Miltonic cadences whose very effect is to convince of the reality of "The One of Fictive Music" so grandly addressed.**

"Peter Quince At The Clavier"

Introduction: There are few poems of Stevens that take narrative form. "The Comedian as the Letter C" is one of the few exceptions, and its narrative is more psychological than real. This poem is another exception. However, the story of Susanna and the Elders is not the subject of the poem; it is used as an illustration to support the subject, which is how beauty and truth are born in the imagination. In this sense "Peter Quince" is another meditation, but one taking the form of **dramatic monologue** with an extensive narrative support.

Summary: A musician plays at a clavier (a keyboard instrument of the piano family). Just as his fingers make music, so there is an interior music of the spirit. This leads him to the conclusion that music is "feeling, not sound." By a rapid transition he equates this to the responsive feeling he experiences for an unnamed woman. This feeling is like that awakened in the Elders by Susanna: "the basses of their beings throb/ In witching chords...."

In the second part, which includes sections II and III, the scene is made immediate. Susanna, having bathed, emerges from her garden bath. But the Elders are spying upon her, and when her maids come they find her crying in her shame.

In the third part, the meaning of this narrative is given: Beauty, as the mind sees it, is transient; its only immortality is in "the flesh." It is flashed into existence by the knowledge of death. It is only when an object "touches the bawdy strings" of man that it reverberates and becomes an object of the imagination. Then such objects receive another kind of "immortality" by the evocation of memory.

Comment: Again Stevens is concerned with exploring the relationship between imagination and reality. In this unusually lyrical piece, full of a rare elegance of phrase and a sensuality quite unique in Stevens, the poet projects himself as the rather naive and lovable clown of Shakespeare, further conceived as a seventeenth century musician. Stevens also, perhaps, expects the reader to recall another famous dramatic monologue in which a musician who considers music as a symbolization of the imaginative powers; Browning's "Abt Vogler." The student might also recall Browning's doctrine of perfection vs. imperfection for useful insights into Stevens' similar ideas.

Form And Style: Formally the poem breaks into two parts. There is a framework of meditation about a highly musical rendering of the story of Susanna and the Elders. Susanna of course was the beautiful woman of the Bible who was deliberately observed bathing naked in her garden by a group of elderly men. This filled her with shame. The scene was a favorite of the artists of the high Renaissance (Titian, Tintoretto, Rembrandt, for example, all rendered it). Of the four parts of the poem, the first two are unrhymed, the second two rhymed. Each section has its own metrical system: the first is made up of five three-lined but metrically systematic stanzas; the second, of four free-verse **stanzas** of varying length; the third, of five rigidly rhymed two-lined stanzas; the fourth, of richly rhymed **couplets** built on an iambic **pentameter** base.

The reader should especially note the great number of words which have to do with music or musical instruments: clavier, keys, sounds, strain, basses, throb, chords, pulse, pizzicati, Hosanna, melody, muted, cymbal, crashed, roaring, horns, noise, tambourines, **refrain**, choral, strings, plays, viol. The student should also notice the considerable number of feminine **rhymes** (two syllables matching): tambourines - Byzantines, portal - immortal, going - flowing, scenting - repenting, auroral - choral, escaping - scraping. These elements contribute in no small measure to the effect of music in the verse.

"Thirteen Ways Of Looking At A Black Bird"

Introduction: Many who do not know any other work of Stevens know this poem. It has appeared in numerous anthologies and in many poetry collections prepared for use in highschools. There are a few ideas the reader ought to remember as he reads it. First of all, it is almost a tour de force of **Imagism**; thirteen times running, taking as his subject blackbirds, the poet presents pictures in which blackbirds occur. In their lack of expository and abstract statements these poems fulfill Pound's demand for a purely pictorial poetry. In a sense too, their form of each verse is close to haiku (the seventeen-syllable Japanese verse pattern which had some influence on Pound, Stevens and other modern poets). Further, its brevity, its adherence to natural images, its **metaphysical** suggestiveness, appeal to poets sick of the lush puddings of sentimentality which most poets of the 1890's were serving. And lastly, the poem is a miracle of improvisation. Stevens was highly skilled in the musical art of improvisation: taking a common **theme** or image, he would exercise his skill as an inventor by showing the numerous ways in which it could be treated. (The most famous example of this ability per se is the incredible "Sea Surface Full of Clouds," but other examples may be found throughout Stevens). The art of the painter and the art of the musician are both visible in Stevens' work.

Summary: In thirteen brief verses, the poet "looks" at the blackbird.

Comment: The blackbird is a fairly common symbol of death. If the reader notes carefully, he will see that there is a plan to the verses: in the first verse the landscape is full of snow, in the succeeding verses there is an implicit movement out of these frozen wastes of winter into spring. Then the poet passes into summer, autumn and again in the last verse to winter. There is a movement also from the emptiness of winter (which for Stevens always symbolized "raw" reality, unimagined and barren) toward - the world as imagined by the creative imagination (VIII-XI) to the world fallen back again, under the influence of death, to what it is without imagination, without men. There are thirteen verses perhaps because thirteen is a number commonly held to be both magical and disastrous. The entire poem treats of Stevens common theme: reality and the imagination, the acceptance of death as a precondition for the knowledge of beauty. The blackbird, death, is always

there. In the solidified and still world of dead winter, his eye moves, watching: "the only moving thing". At the end, under the overcast and snow stuffed sky, he still sits in the cedar tree, from whose wood coffins are traditionally made. To know this is to force one to be real, unsentimental. We will not be like the visionaries of Haddam who waste their lives on illusion; we will see that the blackbird (death) walks about the feet of the women. We will also see that "A man and a woman and a blackbird/ Are one." And finally that, whatever we know, we will know too that "the blackbird (death) is involved" in what we know.

Form And Style: Each verse is **free verse**. The first, second, fifth, eighth, ninth, tenth, and thirteenth are all single sentences. The first, third, ninth, twelfth and thirteenth are pure haiku in mood and structure, although none is written in exactly seventeen syllables. (This is one from Basho, a famous Japanese poet, "From every compass point/ Winds drop cherry petals/ On the holy lake"). The reader ought to note two verses especially. In VIII, Stevens puts his finger on the unique aspect of his poetic genius, his "lucid, inescapable rhythms": these are a gift, however, of his knowledge of the blackbird (death). In verse X, "bawds" are purveyors; in this case it means those "poets" who ignore the real and continue to offer the candied, slick, and empty verse of mere "euphony," nice sounds which say nothing. The **diction** is generally simple.

Question 1: How can the reader be sure that the blackbird is a symbol of death?

Answer: First there is the common association between any bird of black hue and death to support this reading. Ravens, crows, and blackbirds are often associated in superstitious minds with omens of ill luck, disaster, and death. Stevens makes use of this conscious or unconscious association to develop his **theme**. Secondly, the blackbird functions in this poem as death explicitly functions both in "Sunday Morning" ("Death is the mother of beauty") and in the final section of "Peter Quince at the Clavier." Finally, the brooding quality of imminent **catastrophe** which permeates the poem, and which appears more dramatically in verses X and XI, would be inexplicable unless the blackbird symbolized death itself.

Question 2: What is meant by the word "equipage" in XI?

Answer: An "equipage" is simply a carriage with horses and liveried servants.

"The Death Of A Soldier"

Introduction: Many poets, especially in this last hundred years, have taken the deaths of soldiers as occasions for the rhetoric of patriotism. One might recall for instance Horace's Dulce et decorum est pro patria mori ("Sweet and fitting it is to die for the fatherland"), or Brooke's "There is some corner of a foreign field/ That is forever England." Stevens, believing as he did that death was an absolute, could not offer such "illusions." The soldier is one of Stevens' heroes because he is a realist; he looks death in the face, daily without illusion. Still, this is Stevens' hymn of triumph and his memorial to all those who die in battle.

Summary: "The soldier falls." His falling is like autumn, when all life "contracts and death is expected." His fall is part of a universal fall. But he does not become something else because of his death; something grand, heroic, "calling for pomp." "Death is absolute," "without memorial." It is like "autumn" when there is a cessation of the wind. But overhead, the "clouds go, nevertheless, in their direction."

Comment: By this time the reader will be sufficiently familiar with Stevens' principles to understand the poem's meaning almost at first reading. As in "Another Weeping Woman," this poem of death offers absolutely none of the traditional comforts. Stevens, totally consistent to his own principles, may appear hard; it is this terrible hardness, however, that gives to "Another Weeping Woman," "The Snow Man," and "The Death of A Soldier" their tragic grandeur. If they are Greek in their feeling, it is because Stevens, like the Greeks, "saw life steadily and saw it whole." There is very little in American literature or in English literature so lofty, so pure, so absolute in its firm dignity as these memorial poems of Stevens. Even those who do not admit to their basic theological assumptions must feel their grandeur, as one feels the grandeur of the Greek funeral stones without sharing the theological assumptions of the Greeks.

Form And Style: The form is **free verse**, the lines falling and rising through four stanzas; the poet first offers a thesis (first line), then an example of the thesis (second line), then one "happening" itself (third line). By this means he is able to translate back and forth, consequently identify the individual death of the soldier with the common death of the world in autumn, a death in which all life "contracts." The **diction** is, as usual in these early free-verse poems, quite simple.

"Farewell To Florida"

Introduction: In his second book of poems, *Ideas of Order*, Stevens set this poem of renewal and reaffirmation first. Stevens quite early arrived at the conclusion that reality was a neutral, neither organized nor disorganized. Men impose order: poets especially have the task, by their peculiar talent, of seeing ways in which reality can be made orderly for a particular culture. With his usual diffidence, Stevens offers *Ideas of Order*, just as later he will offer "notes" "towards a supreme fiction."

Summary: The poet imagines himself on a ship leaving Key West, Florida, and striking for the North up the Atlantic coast, back to New England. The journey is **metaphysical** and spiritual as well as physical. Like a snake, he has thrown off his old skin. (In "The Comedian as the Letter C" note the line in Part One: "The sea/ Severs not only lands but also selves.") To the north and its "violent mind" he will return.

Comment: Florida and by extension the tropics represent generally in Stevens the rich, fertile, undisciplined and luxurious growths of the imagination. Having indulged so to speak his own imagination, allowing it to spring profusely where it would, he now (in effect) demands a higher discipline of himself. From now on he will demand a sterner, more Euclidean rigidity and logic from his creative self. A number of critics (Ivor Winters for one) have been of the opinion that after *Harmonium* Stevens' poetry fell from the high level which he had so far maintained and became drier, more abstract, less rhythmic. Other critics such as Frank Kermode, (see Bibliography**) maintain that Stevens reaches his greatest height in such later works as Notes towards**

a Supreme Fiction. Certainly Stevens characteristic rhythm, large and musical, changes. He becomes more "statemental," perhaps even didactic. After all, it was his conviction that a major poet had the task of informing the people, which can be another way of saying "giving them form." One thing is certain, however: Stevens never lost his great gifts. It is more true to say he sometimes deliberately suppressed some of them in order to do what he needed to do. During the Thirties, Stevens' kind of poetry was particularly hard-pressed for survival. On every side there was a demand that creative people fit their talents to the tasks of social reorganization. The reader might compare the problems of the pure researcher in science who is hard pressed to prove the usefulness of what he is doing. Stevens knew that what he was doing was useful, but not in the immediately recognizable way that people demanded. Perhaps this is another reason why Stevens became didactic: he was defending his notion of poetry to a hostile world. It is an act which required courage. As he said in "Sailing after Lunch," "But I am, in any case,/ A most inappropriate man/ In a most unpropitious place."

Form And Style: There are four **stanzas** of ten lines each, in iambic **pentameter** erratically rhymed. It is not a **dramatic monologue**, but a personal statement on the poet's part. The image of the ship reminds one of Whitman's "Sail on, sail on, oh ship of state." Stevens was a fervent admirer of the older poet, and we may say that here there is some direct Whitmanian influence on him. The **diction** is quite simple.

The Man With The Blue Guitar

Introduction: The long poem of thirty-three parts is Stevens' first lengthy analysis of the nature and function of poetry. I say "first" because in *Notes Towards a Supreme Fiction*, he was to treat this subject more profoundly, in what one critic (Kermode) considers the greatest long poem of this century. Stevens, as has been pointed out, sees the art of the musician an analogous to the art of the poet. His first book was called *Harmonium*, after a Nineteenth Century keyboard instrument. We have also seen him as Peter Quince at the much older keyboard instrument, the clavier. Now the poet is conceived as a guitarist. We might point out here the color symbolism which runs through the poem. "Blue" is the color of the transforming imagination and of its products. "Green" is the color of the world as it is before being transformed. "Grey" or "white" is the color of "realized" things after they have fallen back; it is the color of poverty, of imagined things which have ceased to have vitality.

Summary: The first section sets the scene. The guitar player (a "shearsman" because like he who shears the wool from a sheep, the poet-player shears reality to the skin and transforms what he shears into "clothing") plays. "The day was green." On his "blue guitar" the green day is transformed, changed. The people complain that "things as they are" are changed by the player, who answers that such is necessarily the case when he plays. But they demand that when he transforms reality he should keep it exactly as they recognize it. The rest of the poem may be taken to be the player's (the poet's) defense and explanation of his art, with some counter-demands and rebuffs from "the people".

In section II, he says that he tries to create a total world, but so far has succeeded in realizing only parts of it; insofar as this is the case, put this defect down to his "blue guitar" - (Stevens own talent and ability).

III is an urgent cry of desire to create the whole man, while at the same time realizing the limitation of his ability.... IV returns to the demand of the people. The poet muses: Is that what life is? "Things as they are?" Should he strive to repeat and mirror the whole of the mass of humanity, its weakness, its strengths, its wrongs and rights as for instance, the contemporary social writers were attempting to see: for example, the poetry of Carl Sandburg and the novels of John Steinbeck, especially *The Grapes of Wrath*).

V is a rejoinder by the people: "Do not speak to us of the greatness of poetry." There is nothing but what we see, what we know. The earth "is flat and bare." Make us a poetry which will be ourselves.

VI is a continuation of the people's demand. The poetry must be "a tune beyond us" but it must be a recreation of "things as they are."

VII is a meditation by the poet. He wishes to be a part of the "sun." (see "Sunday Morning" for the place of the sun in Stevens). Now he "stands in the moon, and calls it good." The sun shares man's work. Not to be a part of the sun is tragic. The thought stills the music of the guitar.

In VIII the poet imagines a storm: the rolling sky and thunder; the clouds vast, touched by light; and his own impotence to recreate it. He strikes the strings discordantly. It is the best he can do.

IX is a continuation of the preceding scene, after the storm. The day is overcast. The player strives to become one with the mood and visible scenery of the day in order to recreate it in music (in poetry). But this "thing" is "yet to be made." It is all like the actor's accoutrements: his costume, his memorized speeches, his practiced gestures, before he takes his place on stage.

X is declamatory and prepares for the arrival of "him whom none believes," the poet (or poetry, or the transforming imagination itself). It is a call to the people; He whom they consider their "adversary" is coming.

XI describes the total transformation of the people and landscape ("Woman become/ The cities, children become the fields/ And men in waves become the sea.") under the influence of "the supreme fiction."

XII. Here the poet identifies himself with his poetry: "Tom-Tom, c'est moi." Tom-Tom is of course the primitive Indian drum, "c'est moi" is French for (literally), "It is I" or as used, "It's me." The whole is the poet, he is the "adversary" of those who demand "things as they are." But where does he "begin and end?" And how can he "declare" those things which are not "himself" (as a private person) and "yet must be?"

XIII is a point of quiet. The poet urges himself to be still. Whatever is not "blue" is a "corrupting pallor." "Be content," he urges himself, to be the "center of the world/ Of blue...."

XIV. The world lies in its dimensions, transformed. The light, the illumination, of the poetic imagination searches out, finds, and bathes the universe. The rest is darkness, and half light.

XV. The poet looks at a picture by Picasso (probably *Guernica*, the tortured, twisted, deformed, fragmentation of the world painted to memorialize the Spanish Civil War) and wonders, is this "a picture of ourselves?" Is he, the poet (Stevens) "a man that is dead?" Is everything he imagines he sees "a memory" and not really there? Is he the one living in illusion?

XVI. His thought is bitter. The earth, then, is not a "mother," but merely stone, stone which begrudges human existence, "an oppressor." There is nothing left for lovers but to die.

XVII. The bitter thoughts continue. Man is nothing, an animal that dies. Under his grave mound he rots. The guitar too is a mound. There is no reason to expect life through poetry. Even the trumpeting north wind is only "a worm composing on a straw."

XVIII. Slowly the bitterness dies away. Society is chaos, the world is hellish, yet sometimes "After long strumming on certain nights" one begins to see "a dream...in which/ I can believe."

XIV. What the poet must do is subjugate the "monster" which reality is, make it himself, and "play of the monster and of myself."

XX. "What is there in life except one's ideas?" the poet asks. This is what he believes. What is analogous to the state of belief? "Believe would be a brother full/ Of love, believe would be a friend...." And so, not having this, the poet is sad; he cannot play.

In XXI, a note of greater assertion is sounded. The self is "a substitute for all the gods." One's self and one's land are enough, "as they are."

XXII. This is a direct statement of what poetry is, how it functions. Poetry is itself. It goes out from and returns to itself. Between the issuance and the return, there is "An absence of reality" or "Things as they are." But need this be so? Would it be better, truer to say that poetry is the movement back and forth, the landscape giving something to the imagination, the imagination giving something to the landscape, in a "universal intercourse"?

XXIII. The poet transforms the idea set forth in section XXII into symbolic form as a duet between the poet and "the undertaker", death. Poetry then is a harmony achieved between opposites - the vulgar and the sublime, life and death, order and disorder - an achievement of stability which is enjoyable.

XXIV. A poem is something found. It is the meeting between the object which everyone has ignored or discarded, and the very person for whom it is precious.

XXV. The poet imagines himself as a magician in robes with the symbols of his office, balancing the world on his nose and swaying to a dance. He twirls and spins the world every which way. The inhabitants of the world do not know that it is spun by the magician. On it the grass "turns green" and then "gray." But the nose (the magician) is still there. The transformations of the magician (the poet) will be the "things as they are" of the future: i.e., when people see the world as the poet sees it.

XXVI. For the poet the world is "washed in his imagination." It is a "giant that fought/ Against the murderous alphabet": i.e., the language of the poet which will subdue the world. (Compare "The Plot Against the Giant.")

XXVII. The sea is conceived as the shifting, ever-changing movements of reality. "Geographers and philosophers" (who try to fix reality immutably) are ridiculed by the sea: it cannot be mapped - no more than reality. Still, one must live with it. Icebergs for instance are like those who "tour to shift the shifting scene" because they cannot accept the "self" (see XXI).

XXVIII. "I am a native in this world," the poet declares, and as such "think in it as a native thinks." The landscape gives me strength. "Things are as I think they are/ And say they are on the blue guitar." (It is, in a sense, a final answer).

XXIX. The poet recalls that he once visited a cathedral. For him everything was false. But for the inhabitants of that cathedral it was the real. A man and his landscape are one.

XXX. So the poet, who in II could not create but the fragments of a man, now, having found his solution, fashions "a man." It is himself: odd, but observant. He observes the telephone poles, the cables, the "banal suburb" of Oxidia (a made-up name suggesting both Acadia: ennui, boredom; and Oxville: a place inhabited by dense, slow-witted creatures), where everything is purchased on the installment plan and beyond which lie smoke stacks and machines. But this is what is "there." From Oxidia, he, the poet, must start; it is the seed. Oxidia for him "is Olympia" (the Greek mountain on which the gods assembled).

XXXI. One would wish it were different, but one must start with what is, "things as they are." Employer combats employee, the nerves will be distraught, the noises of the day will intrude; but "It must be this rhapsody or none,/ The rhapsody of things as they are."

XXXII. The poet urges (the people) to throw away their preconceptions of what "things are," the definitions, the "rotted names." Once the world is met with the "crusts" of it (which one carries stale in one's mind) destroyed, "the blue guitar surprises you."

XXXIII. Stevens concludes on a note of high affirmation. We must throw off "that generation's dream"; it is gone "in the mud, in Monday's dirty light." It was the "only dream they knew." It is not ours. "Here" is our dream - "the bread to come." We must have our own dream, our own world, and our poetry will provide us with it: our "imagined pine," our "imagined joy."

> **Comment: A poet presents his arguments, not to the reasoning intellect but to the responsive imagination of his audience. Any paraphrase will, therefore, be an inadequate reduction of the power and subtlety, and possibly a distortion, of these arguments. However, I think it possible, and necessary, to offer the general scaffolding of the ideas, implicit and explicit, offered us in "The Man with the Blue Guitar." Briefly, they run as follows: "Things as they are" represent the sum of the real as any culture sees it and believes it to be. But, what it sees and how it sees it is a result of how it was "imagined" at some former time. In other words, there is a time lag. The result of this time lag is that the people and the poet see the world in different ways. The poet sees things, because of his peculiar talent and gifts, as they "really are." The poet therefore seems to "change" "things as they are" when he recreates them in his poetry. But "things as they are" for the poet will be the "things as they are" for the people of the future. They are "the bread of the future."**

In "The Man with the Blue Guitar", Stevens is teaching his audience the relationship between poetry and reality. He says rather explicitly that there is a "universal intercourse" between the landscape and the imagination of man, one bringing the other into being in a symbiotic relationship, each sustained by the other. The constructions of vision are adequate to their own time and place. That is why the "dream" of the past is no longer valid; it is gone "in the mud, in Monday's dirty light." The man of imagination (the poet, the musician, the hero, the sun, the owl) has the courage, the strength and the corrected sensibility to see the world as it "really is."

During the thirties (as has been pointed out in another connection) there was an almost universal demand for the artist to put his talent at the service of causes. The student might give further attention to Stevens' position in this matter: he abhorred the topical, and repudiated the propagandistic servilitude to which art was being put. A further treatment of this theme may be found in "Reply to Papini" and *Owl's Clover*. It is a curious paradox that Stevens, who on the surface seems to be the most elegant and esthetic of poets, should have produced such a body of sustained social and political criticism. But unlike the social and political criticism of most poets, it can be read with profit by mature citizens.

Form And Style: There are thirty-three sections, recalling Dante's divisions of his *Divine Comedy* into three sections of thirty-three each. Generally the meter is iambic **tetrameter**, but there is considerable variation in this (as for instance in V which is, perhaps, best defined as iambic **pentameter**). Most of the sections are made up of two-line stanzas, though this also may vary: i.e., some have six, others seven stanzas. More than half of these lines are rhymed; rhyme however seems rather an accidental than a formal structural element in the poem. Within these basic patterns, the poet is able to command a number of tones: descriptive, bemused, angry, ironic, satiric, commanding, melancholic, confused, ringing, self-critical, challenging, visionary, savage. His rhythms range from those of the cryptic axiom, through the Swiftian snarl, to lines of Miltonic splendor, to lines which can only be described as couched in the interior rhythms of the meditating mind.

The **diction** is almost uniformly simple, even colloquial: "twang," "ai-yi-yi". (Stevens says that this last was a common expression of joy among the Pennsylvania Dutch of his boyhood). Some words may require explication: "fantoche" of XXX is an Italian puppet; "aviled" means made vile.

Question 1: Stevens assumes many masks (the middle-aged, monocled dandy of "Le Monocle de Mon Oncle" and the "rabbi" of the same poem; the citizen instructor of *Notes Towards a Supreme Fiction*; Peter Quince; the "inchling" bantam of "Bantams in Pine-Woods"). What mask or masks, if any, does he assume in "The Man with the Blue Guitar."?

Answer: Stevens assumes one sustained mask throughout: "The Man with the Blue Guitar," that of the guitar player himself. The mask of the musician was particularly congenial to Stevens; not only did he see the task of the composer as analogous to the task of the poet, he incorporated many musical devices into his craft (improvisation, variation, counterpoint, **refrain**, melodic transformation and repetition, etc.). Here, because he is particularly concerned with the task of the American poet as against the poet generally, his musician plays a common

American instrument, the guitar (as against the British harmonium, the baroque (17th-18th Century) clavier.

The persona or mask of the guitar player is not, however, the only mask which Stevens assumes, although it is the most important one. In XXV he assumes the mask of the conjuror, the musician, the shaman, or to put it as Stevens wished it to be understood: the primitive poet, or "maker" - one who makes worlds. (In ancient cultures the poet was god-inspired; he gave people the god's word; he gave people the law; he wore the symbols, marks, and signs of his office; as a conjuror he called up the god; he knew the past, the present, and the future.)

Another mask is constructed before our eyes: "old fantoche" is the poet as puppet, the "evolved" man, the constructed man of XXX. And, finally, there are the briefer, but no less important identifications of the poet with the musical instrument itself ("Tom-tom, c'est moi," and "The Blue guitar/ And I are one.").

Question 2: What does Stevens mean by the line "Oxidia is Olympia" in XXX?

Answer: The poet identified Oxidia as the landscape available to him as a poet. It is the "banal suburb," it is vulgar and sooty and industrialized. He paints a savagely satiric picture of its inhabitants (oxlike, boorish, mannerless, un-aspiring, surrounded by smokestacks, machines, and row after row of barrack like prefabricated, cookie-cut houses purchased on the installment plan). But, he says, this is "his" landscape; to deny it, to dream like the peacock of beautiful places is to build castles in Spain. The poet must accept what is his. Then just as the poets of Greece created, out of their relationship to its landscape, Olympia - home of the gods, but also the gods themselves - he must create out of Oxidia whatever "paradise" he can. So "Oxidia is Olympia." This insistence on the vital relationship between poet and landscape is one of the essentials of Stevens' thought.

A Later Poem: "The Well Dressed Man With A Beard"

Introduction: As he grew older, Stevens continued to write poetry. *The Collected Poems* was published in conjunction with the celebration of his seventy-fifth birthday. In this he included all the poems which he estimated were vital elements of his poetic "world" or mundus. This volume he wished, at first, to call *The Whole of Harmonium*. But he continued to produce poetry. *Opus Posthumous* includes such later poems, as well as many, that for one reason or another, had not been included in *The Collected Poems*. The poems discussed here are not as well known as those analyzed in the previous portion of this book, but are in the opinion of many critics among the major achievements of this poet.

Stevens' conviction that man's existence is limited by this life appears to many readers, and sometimes to Stevens himself, as pessimism and despair. How can a man survive, be joyful, productive, and content if he is convinced there is nothing beyond this, the visible? The reader will recall that such is the cause of the lady's anxiety in "Sunday Morning"; she demanded an "imperishable bliss." The poet then proceeded to demonstrate that "imperishable" and "bliss" were mutually annihilating conceptions. There he also spoke of the multitudinous delights of the physical world, the only world we know. In this small poem, "The Well Dressed Man with a Beard", the same notion in the subject: The capacity of the "thing" itself to satisfy, is used.

Summary: The voice (presumably attached to the well-dressed, bearded man of the title) proceeds with calm assurance: "After the final no there comes a yes", he says. Even if all things (the visible world) vanished in some **catastrophe** or in impersonal annihilation (for it is the same thing to Stevens that the world disappear for the speaker as for the speaker to disappear for the world), there is one thing remaining and that one thing is "enough." The visible is so vast, and one needs but one "thing" to make a douce campagna" (lovely countryside); at this thought the voice begins to multiply this conception of delight at the notion. Then it breaks off, saying only: "It can never be satisfied, the mind, never."

> **Summary: The thought, "the idea," of this poem is consistent with the total body of Stevens work. Essentially he is merely saying again that the visible is enough: it provides unending delights for the mind of the beholder. From the minutest payment of existence, for example, the sounding of the little cricket's horn, one gets sustenance and satisfaction. The implication of the first line adds, however, a new element to Stevens; the element of despair overcome with particular force. Unsustained by "paradise" or the ignorant enthusiasm of youth, the mind of the aging man-poet moves toward cynicism, and finally meets despair. At this point many have stopped, contemplating many types of suicide, real and symbolic. But Stevens pushes beyond: "After the final no there comes a yes." The courage which had led him toward nihilism yielded a further positive fruit of joy. This voice, though allied to "Uncle's" of "Le Monocle de Mon Oncle," is not ironic; it shares Uncle's maturity and age and elegance, but not his doubt. "No was the night. Yes is the present sun." He sleeps at night, and without nightmares.**

Form And Style: The form is **blank verse**: that is, unrhymed iambic **pentameter**. The title suggests that there is a persona, or mask of the poet, but this is hardly a **dramatic monologue**. Primarily it is, like so much of Stevens, a meditation. It is interesting to see how naturally and easily Stevens translates intellectual conceptions into concrete images. The first two lines are statement; the sentence is a conclusion. Typically the rest of the poem is an analysis and demonstration of the initially stated conclusion. This practice, it might be noted, is unusual in modern poetry. Most modern poets (Yeats, Eliot, Robert Lowell, for example) start with the concrete and conclude with a statement (implicit or explicit) which is the "meaning" of the poem. This is called inductive procedure; the reader is given the evidence, and then the conclusion. Stevens' procedure is often deductive: that is, he gives the conclusion, and then the evidence. Here, in the present poem, we must note how the calm, convinced tone of the first few lines begins to rise in intensity: This intensity is itself the rhythmic and imagistic equivalent of the joy which led to the conclusion. In other words, the evidence is not simply "given" the reader, it is made part of his own experience. Having, by the very act of reading the poem, shared Stevens' experience, he is prepared to accept the initial statement as valid. When the reader comes to the lines beginning "Ah! douce campagna," he is caught up in a series of short, passionate phrases, in a rush of images of such beauty and accuracy, that it is as if he were being lifted on a series of higher-and higher-rising waves. Beyond this he cannot go. And so, form following function, the poet stops, inserting three dots to indicate that the series of ascending waves is eternal. Hence, the final assertion: the mind can never be satisfied, except by annihilation.

The vocabulary is simple and precise. Following his usual freedom of practice, Stevens does not hesitate to use the "hierophantic phrase" (see Part III: "Stevens and the Critics") in "douce campagna." Here "douce campagna" is to be taken as one more synonym for the "invented world", the "mundus," the "supreme fiction," all of which terms we have discussed before. The Italian expression has the effect here of enlarging the meaning of the poem. The reader is expected to be reminded of the pastoral tradition of poetry and the "invented world", - "the lovely landscape" of Arcadia. Arcadia is, of course, another equivalent for Oxidia and Olympia (see the Comment on "The Man with the Blue Guitar"). "Aureole" is a halo of light here. Medieval and Renaissance practice was to picture the saints with such halos or aureoles of light about their heads, and sometimes, bodies, to symbolize that such persons had attained completeness, perfection, paradise - what Stevens would have thought the state of being in his "supreme fiction."

Question 1: What is meant by the phrase "honey in the heart"? "Green in the body"?

Answer: The phrase, "honey in the heart", means the inmost, sweetest kernel of joy to be found disclosed in any contemplated thing. In the rotted tree, in jars or the skull of the lion (so tradition has it) the bees built hives and yield them honey. To find such honey is exquisite and rare joy. But, Stevens says, any "thing" in the visible world, loved, sought, and found, will yield this honey: not a honey for the mouth, but a honey in the heart of existence itself, for the heart of the beholder. Such honey, therefore, is food for the mind. "Green in the body," has exactly the same force. Green is the color of growth. The mind, fed by honey, the body, flourishing green. It might be noted that in this and similar poems ("The World as Mediation," "Of Mere Being," "Reality is An Activity of the Most August Imagination") Stevens is assimilated into the long tradition of mystics, all of whom, in one way or another, held that through the contemplation of the visible the invisible is disclosed (see Martz in Bibliography for a fuller analysis of this aspect of Stevens.)

Question 2: Why does Stevens end his poem by saying: "It can never be satisfied, the mind, never."?

Answer: He ends with this statement because it sums up his consistent position from at least "Sunday Morning" on. If the mind can be satisfied, then it is dead. It is no longer capable of participating in the "marriage of flesh and air" (see Comment on "Oklahoma"). If the mind is satisfied, it means that like the geographers and philosophers of "The Man with the Blue Guitar," it has settled for maps and systems instead of what is "there": reality shifts, it is a moving sea of the visible. It can never be mapped, for it is always changing. To be "satisfied" is to settle for maps of the thing instead of a continuously vital relationship with the "the honey of the thing". Therefore the mind cannot - must not-be satisfied: "never."

Some Final Poems

Introduction: Here we will consider collectively a group of poems which Stevens wrote during the last fifteen years of his life; that is, from the time he was sixty or more years until his death. We will consider "The Good Man Has No Shape," "A Primitive Like an Orb," "An Ordinary Evening in New Haven," "Final Soliloquy of the Interior Paramour," "A Child Asleep in Its Own Life," "As You Leave The Room" and "Of Mere Being." These are, of course, by no means the most important, nor for that matter, least important poems of the group. For the fact of the matter is that in his final verse, Stevens reaches a profundity of thought and elasticity and simplicity of **diction** which many critics believe to be (aside from Shakespeare and Milton) one rarely matched in English Literature. These poems have been chosen only because in them Stevens makes explicit statements, or treats his central **theme** in such a way, as to make his "ideas" more available to the student.

Summaries And Analyses: In "The Good Man had No Shape" Stevens makes more clear his conception of what the good man is, and this conception is logically connected with his whole notion of the relationship between reality and the imaginative and the poet. The poet is never in Stevens merely one who uses words, nor for that matter is he to be identified with the artist generally. All men of imagination, who (like the "Snowman" and the "hero" - the sun) see the world undistorted and without illusion are "good." His function is to be a standard for others; he has courage because it requires courage to look undisturbed on the real. **Convention** provides us with illusions, systems which keep us from facing "things as they are." "If the good man "has no shape" it is because he never is "satisfied," therefore does not systematize himself and define himself by edges and limits. The good man like the sunlight has no shape: he gives reality (like light) its shape. But Stevens ends the poem with the phrase "as if they knew." For ultimately, one cannot ever make the dogmatic statement about the good man that "he has no shape." He, perhaps, has, but that shape is one not discernible except by other "good" men.

In "A Primitive Like an Orb," Stevens offers another of his many analogies for the function of the poet with regard to the real. In this meditation, the poet makes the assertion (part VII) that there is one "central poem" of which all poems are a part. This central poem is the "supreme fiction," The "Giant" reality, who is ever and always changing; the "ultimate reality" with which imagination "marries."

In 'An Ordinary Evening in New Haven," Stevens continues in a long poem of eleven parts, the analysis of the poet's function. It is set in the poet's own city ("Oxidia" if you know New Haven). The poet searches for reality. An effete academician (Professor Eucalyptus) suggests that the search for reality is "as momentous as/ The search for god. In spite of the satiric name, Stevens is not using his statement satirically. The point for Stevens is not that the search for reality is the search for "God"; moreover, reality is not searched for, it is found. The poem is, it is reality. The "great poem", "the supreme fiction, reality itself" is: the individual poem is "the cry of its occasion." It is part of the "world." But the poem changes "things as they are." "Oxidia" is moved toward "Olympia." (See Comment on "The Man with the Blue Guitar.")

"The Final Soliloquy of the Interior Paramour" connects with "To the One of Fictive Music." (See Summary and Comment on that poem.) The one who has all his life been the poet's friend and the object of his love speaks. It is her final speech, because the poet whom she inhabits is old and near death. Here, for the first time she (the muse, Stevens himself) make definite what has been more or less implicit throughout Stevens' work: "We say God and the imagination are one." It is a sad, and slow and utterly dignified poem, which with the few others still to be discussed makes the reader realize the terrible suffering spirit which the poet endured, and the great pride which survived against incredible odds. We are reminded of Whitman's last poem, "Goodbye, My Fancy."

In "A Child Asleep in Its Own Life,"' The poet, in an extremely brief, simple, and profound poem, says in effect, there are many old men, you know them, you pass them on the street or sitting on park benches, but among them is one "that broods on all the rest." In fact all things exist only because that old man's mind imagines them; to him the world is a dream which he, the poet, the old man, "realizes." He never grows old, he is, in fact, a child asleep. But more he is "sole emperor" of what you are. Remembering that "emperor" (in "The Emperor of Ice-Cream") has been identified by Stevens as Death, there is a certain warning note implied here: "when the poet's world" ceases, dies, "things as they are" will vanish too. The verse continues the tone of great pride found in the previous one.

"As You Leave the Room" is Stevens' farewell. Sad, profound, unblinking, he faces now at the end of his long life the possibility that all his life he has been wrong. He touches allusively, on some of his famous poems. It he is a "skeleton," these poems are not what "skeletons" think about. Has all his life been wasted in this single-minded dedication to poetry, to the "supreme fiction," to the analysis of the relation between imagination and reality? Has he been wrong to "disbelieve" in the reality available to him from the past? No, no, he can "touch" his world, touch it "every way." It exists, therefore he exists. It is; he is real. And still "nothing has been changed "except that the "unreal" things have been changed: they have been "realized." And yet, because once a thing has been "realized" people forget that it was ever "unreal," it is "as if nothing had been changed at all." On this note the poet reaches his final remarks on the activity of the poet: he makes the "unreal" real.

"Of Mere Being" is perhaps the last poem Stevens wrote. It is, like some of the final poem of Yeats, mystical, enigmatic, mysterious. Near death, his imagination pushes to the ultimate limits, to "the palm at the end of the mind/ Beyond the last thought." There is a bird, gold-feathered, who sings "a foreign song. It is foreign because what it sings has no "human meaning" no "human feeling." To hear it singing makes one happy. But the bird does not sing for the purpose of making his listeners happy. He does not relate to them at all. He sings because he must. He is the poet, the songs are his poems. He does not "mean," he "is." And so, Stevens, to the very last, demanded respect for the integrity of his function. The poet who could not and would not compromise by writing of "things as they are" offers himself - like Yeats in "Sailing to By-zantium" - in the figure of the bird, a golden bird, who sings because he must. The last **stanza** in its three lines of three imagistic statements, offers the final view of the poet. The palm on which the bird sings stands "on the edge of space." Stevens had always worked on the frontiers of sensibility, at that edge of the real which borders on the "unreal." Always he, likes his ancestors, was a pioneer, bringing into the domain of the imagination the huge continent of America, of the modern world. But now the wind moves slowly in the branches, recalling the final verse of "Thirteen Ways of Looking at a Blackbird," where, when the wind moves in the snowy landscape, the crow (death) will rise slowly and make his way to his assignation. The bird's "fire-fangled (from "new-fangled": made, constructed, touched by fire) "feathers dangle down." The bird (the poet) droops, is dying. Shortly after writing this, Stevens died.

Question: Why is it valid to say that the conclusion "God and the imagination are one" had been implicit in his work from the beginning?

Answer: It is valid because a close reading even of the poetry of *Harmonium* shows it to be so. In "Sunday Morning" for instance, Stevens denies the validity of the lady's religion, goes on to identify "love" with the "supreme fiction" which in itself (in "A High-Toned Old Christian Woman") is identified with "poetry." In the second poem, he equates the old woman's notion of God with the "supreme fiction." He is not saying, it seems to me, that God is a product of man's imagination pure and simple. What he is saying is that "the giant," the grand, "the central poem" is what the "hero" and the "good man" constantly seek. "Reality," "God," imagination interact, interpenetrate, sustain one another in this sense, and this sense is, for Stevens, the only real sense: "God and the imagination are one." In the oldest sense of the word, Stevens is a religious poet. What he fought was illusion, not vision. Like most great poets he believes first in his intuitions: like most great poets he assimilates the mystic tradition and asserts that, far from being fragmented, and unknowable, reality is one: single, continuous and entire. Imagination, in its grandest sense is realization of "the central poem"; this "central poem" is also "God." Therefore "God and the imagination are one."

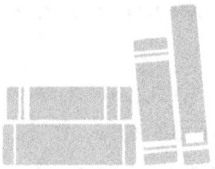

INTRODUCTION TO WALLACE STEVENS

CRITICISM

Of all the poets, recognizably major, who have written in English in the Twentieth Century, Stevens has received the least critical attention. Were we to compare, for instance, the number of books and articles, lectures and courses devoted to Eliot, Yeats, Frost, Pound - against all of whom Stevens may be weighed in the balance and not found wanting - with the number devoted to Stevens, it would be possible to see how true this is. There are indications, however, that this error of attention is being redressed. Aside from a few scattered and isolated references through the twenties, thirties, and early forties, proportionally much the greater number of analyses of and commentaries on Stevens have been published since the fifties. There is every reason to believe that this interest will continue and increase; the very reasons which kept American critics in the past from considering him are, paradoxically, those which make him so valuable an object of critical attention today: as Henry Wells says in his excellent book, *Introduction to Wallace Stevens*: "He is more thoughtful, imaginative, and elegant, not to mention profound, than most or possibly any of his contemporaries." These are the qualities which measure cultural maturity; insofar as critics find them worthwhile, our culture may be said to be more mature.

REASONS FOR A DEARTH OF CRITICISM

Still, there are a number of reasons why it was only late in life and after his death that the poet became the object of critical attention. First of all, although he had been publishing single pieces for quite some time in the little magazines, Stevens did not publish his first book until he was well into his forties. Certainly he was known among a small group of fellow poets, but his natural diffidence, his life-long avoidance of - as Wells puts it - "promiscuous conversation on literary topics," kept him rather a mystery. By the time Stevens had published his first book, T. S. Eliot, his younger contemporary, had already begun to acquire an international reputation. Stevens' abhorrence of publicity was total; it was only towards the end of his full life that he chose to speak, though rarely, in public forums. I don't think there is on record any interview with him, although there are recorded many with his contemporaries. Certainly this lack of desire, this absolute distaste for self-advertisement accounts in great measure for the dearth of criticism about him. Stevens was of the opinion that his poetry should make its own way, without introduction by him or fanfare or advertisement. And it has.

A BAD TIME

The second reason is more complex. Stevens published one book in the twenties, *Harmonium*. It sold very few copies. He did not publish his second collection until the thirties. During the thirties he published with increasing frequency. The times were, to put the case mildly, unpropitious. It was not mere whimsey which led Stevens to call himself "A most inappropriate man/ In a most inauspicious place." During the thirties, after the apparent collapse of the American capitalistic system, the general cry on all sides was for social reorganization. Everywhere, in that grey decade, fear and panic demanded radical, and therefore easy, solutions to complicated social and economic problems. It was the kind of period when people ignore the complexities of life, insist on simple answers, and say "Are you with me or against me?" They demanded of intellectuals commitment; of artists, the service of their talents, but they didn't know much about how art works. In this atmosphere of demand, Stevens chose to stand aloof because he recognized that poetry can serve no master, neither the Right nor the Left. Therefore whatever critical attention Stevens got in the thirties was apt to be negative, denigrating, and unsympathetic. When the social conditions which had made for this response changed, so did the intellectual and critical conditions. The poet who was called a-social, ivory-towerish, and aloof turned out to have contributed a sounder and more complete analysis of the social complexities of his time than many of his contemporaries (see Chapter Twelve of Wells' *Introduction*). But as late as 1960, like a conditioned reflex, Stevens' *Opus Posthumous* was reviewed in The New Leader as having an air of "chic" and "conspicuous consumption," deserving only "posh epithets."

A DIFFICULT ART

But the final reason is the difficulty of Stevens' art, the demand he puts upon the reader, the continuous chastity of his **diction** and **imagery**. As Wells says: "His art is to a surprising degree new, even in its peculiar blending of new and old. And new things almost always present stubborn obstacles." To those - the majority - habituated to the old ("things as they are"), Stevens' unique combination of manner and matter has often been too great a barrier to overcome. They refused to see or could not see what he was doing, hear what he was saying. As John Enck puts it, for them Stevens becomes "a self-conscious clown trapped in a gray flannel suit, an uneasy apologist for his capitalistic values, a holiday literature dangling contrived snippets, a provincial who relieves tedium through exotic phantasies, or an amateur of five-finger exercises...."

STEVENS AS IMAGIST

In the earliest days it was characteristic practice to place Stevens with the Imagist school in America: Richard Aldington, William Carlos Williams, Ezra Pound, Amy Lowell. Enck says that "Stevens never abandoned this technique" of **Imagism**. In this Stevens "unquestionably belongs to his era, as any memorable artist does, if only because he rejects his immediate predecessors' cliches." Stevens himself both accepted the fact that the poet must be "modern," "a poet of the present time," and also the need to transcend: "One cannot spend one's time in being modern when there are so many more important things to be." Again Imagism, as Stevens knew, was merely one technique of poetry, "an ancient phase of poetry." Although Stevens practiced the imagist mode to the end, it was not out of habit merely, but because it was one of the techniques of his craft.

STEVENS, AMERICAN

"Because of his distinctive style," says Enck, "Stevens' reputation... still rests pejoratively on idiosyncratic syllables." In fact Stevens commands not one special and exotic style, but one which ranges, for example "from rustic to urban, colloquial to formal, drably seen to vividly invented, transitory to permanent.... His vocabulary becomes a genuinely American idiom." Stevens, in defense of his own practice of never keeping a word out of his "invented world" simply because it wasn't Anglo-Saxon, says: "If a poem seems to require a hierophantic phrase, that phrase should pass. This is a way of saying that one of the consequences of the ordination of style is not to limit it, but to enlarge it, to enrich and liberate it." When asked whether American elements ought to be emphasized by artists in their work, Stevens said: "An American has to be an American because there is nothing else for him to be." The critic Harry Levin, in the Harvard Advocate, once remarked on Stevens stylistic omnivorousness: "Apparently he can absorb the extremes of patois and anarchism without the slightest effort." Doubtless the finest analysis and most persistent and wide - ranging defense (or explanation) of Stevens' style is to be found in John Enck's *Wallace Stevens* (see Bibliography), which is perhaps in spite of its author's own fondness for the hierophantic phrase the fullest treatment of Stevens now available to the student.

STEVENS' "IDEAS"

The early critics, conditioned not to expect ideas from poets, were usually satisfied to stop at the surface of Stevens' work, to praise or condemn his manner. But if manner and matter can be separately considered, Stevens' primary concern was not with the first but with the second. "To all appearances," says Henry Wells in *Introduction to Wallace Stevens*, "he was born both a poet and a philosopher in aesthetics... His poetry at times grew too philosophical and lost its spontaneity; his philosophy at times grew too vague and lost its cutting, rational edge." But for all that, like the Latin philosopher Lucretius, Stevens was both

AN INTRODUCTION OF WALLACE STEVENS

one and the other. "For a lifetime Stevens was engaged in his priestly task of expounding the relations of art and reality." Some have condemned the Stevens of *Harmonium* as too dandiacal and rococo and unreal - too frivolous; others, and often the same ones, have condemned the work after *Harmonium* as too abstract, too difficult, too inhuman, too "serious". Some denied he was a poet at all. Against the charge of his "inhumanity," Wells says "he is, in fact, one of the most lusty, robust, and firm-grained writers in American literature, and perhaps the most gifted of all in expressing the joy of life." The student who is interested in pursuing Stevens' "ideas" further should devote his attention first to Frank Kermode's *Wallace Stevens* which presents in more or less chronological order Stevens' thought as it is presented in both the prose and the poetry. Next, he ought to turn to Wells' Introduction which considers Stevens under such aspects as "Psychological Insights," "The Psychology of Art," and "The Nature of Art." Wells also isolates certain persistent "ideas" of Stevens for special analysis (for instance, "The Hero"). Next, the student ought to devote his attention to Enck's *Wallace Stevens*, which, though difficult, rewards by its constant insights.

UNSYMPATHETIC CRITICS

The critics so far considered have been sympathetic. The student should be aware that such weighty critics as John Crowe Ransom, Yvor Winters, and Allen Tate (see Bibliography) have made negative evaluations of Stevens. The main charge has been Stevens' "abstractness," his "inhumanity," his "preciosity," his "diffidence." It is to these charges that the critics mentioned above have directed themselves in the works cited. With one charge, however, they do not, nor perhaps can they, deal. This is Yvor Winter's charge (see Bibliography), that having written (in "Sunday Morning") one of the great poems of the English language, Stevens deteriorated as a poet. The reason for this deterioration, insofar as one can read Winters clearly, seems to be Stevens' lack of moral commitment. Winters believes, and rightly so, that there is some connection between a man's style and his belief; that for instance, an insecure man will display an insecure style, a man of conviction a firm style. But this kind of criteria for evaluating really assumes, for one, that there is an absolute relationship between style and creed; and two, that the critic's own credal credentials are themselves absolutely valid. In a sense, Winters seems to have mistaken stylistic daring for moral disarray; he seems to make it a condition of excellence that a poet be an orthodox Christian.

But surely the answer to this is that any poet must first be an orthodox poet. Winters criticism is really an attack on Stevens' romanticism and on his belief that truth is not a universal, but is relative to individuals in the context of their time and place.

There is no kind of real answer to such criticism except perhaps this from Wells: "He writes with complete integrity, for the enlargement of his reader's heart, mind, and pleasure, not for the convenience of his reviewers, critics, or apologists."

BIBLIOGRAPHICAL MATERIAL

As has been pointed out (see Introduction), the facts of Stevens' life are scanty. We will have to wait for the publication of Samuel French Morse's biography for the full treatment. In the meantime there is available the material in Morse's two "Introductions" (to *Selected Poems* and *Opus Posthumous*); in Kermode's first chapter, "Life", and in *Historical Review of Berks County* (see Bibliography).

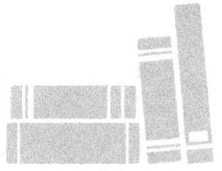

BIBLIOGRAPHY

WORKS BY WALLACE STEVENS

Verse

Harmonium. New York, 1923; New York 1931.

Ideas of Order. New York, 1935 (Alcestis Press); New York, 1936 (Knopf).

Owl's Clover. New York, 1936.

The Man with the Blue Guitar and Other Poems. New York, 1937.

Parts of a World. New York, 1942.

Notes Towards a Supreme Fiction. Cummington (Massachusetts), 1944.

Esthetique du Mal. Cummington Massachusetts, 1944.

Transport to Summer. New York, 1947.

A Primitive Like an Orb. New York, 1948.

The Auroras of Autumn. New York, 1950.

Selected Poems". London, 1953.

Collected Poems. New York, 1954 (Knopf).

Collected Poems. London, 1955 (Faber).

Opus Posthumous. Poems, Plays, Prose by Wallace Stevens. Edited, with an Introduction, by Samuel French Morse. New York, 1957 (Knopf).

Opus Posthumous. London, 1959 (Faber).

Poems, Selected, and with an introduction by S. F. Morse. New York 1959 (Vintage Books).

Prose

The Necessary Angel. **New York, 1951. This includes the following:**

"The Noble Rider and the Sound of Words," published originally in *The Language of Poetry*, ed. Allen Tate, Princeton, 1942;

"The Figure of the Youth as Virile Poet," originally published in *Sewanee Review*, LII (1944):

"Three Academic Pieces," originally published in *Partisan Review*, XV (1947) also Cummington Press (Mass. 1947):

"About One of Marianne Moore's Poems," originally published in Quarterly Review of Literature, IV (1948);

"Effects of Analogy," first appearing in Yale Review, XXXVIII (1948);

"Imagination as Value," first in *English Institute Essays 1948*, New York (1949);

"The Relations Between Poetry and Painting," *Museum of Modern Art*, New York 1951.

The Necessary Angel. London, 1960 (Faber).

Opus Posthumous. New York, 1957. Includes: *Adagia* (a collection of prose axioms from his notebooks); "A Collect of Philosophy"; "Two or Three Ideas"; "The Irrational Element in Poetry"; sixteen short prose pieces.

Opus Posthumous. London, 1959.

BOOKS AND ARTICLES ON WALLACE STEVENS

Alvarez, A. *The Shaping Spirit*, London, 1958.

Benamon, M. "Le **Theme** du Heros dans la Poesie de Wallace Stevens," *Etudes Anglais*, XII (1959), 222-230.

Bewler, Marius. *The Complete Fate*, London, 1952.

Blackmuir, R. P. *Form and Value in Modern Poetry*, New York, 1957.

Doggett, Frank. "Wallace Stevens' Later Poetry," *English Literary History*, XXV (1958), 137-154.

Donoghue, Denis. *The Third Voice*, Princeton, 1959.

Ellman, R. "Wallace Stevens' Ice-Cream," *Kenyon Review*, XIX (1957) 89-105.

Enck, John J. *Wallace Stevens: Images and Judgments, Illinois, 1964.*

Ford, Charles Henri. "Verlaine in Hartford," *View*, I (1940).

Frankenberg, Lloyd. *Pleasure Dome.* Cambridge (Massachusetts) 1949.

Fraser, G. S. "Mind All Alone," *New Statesman*, 9 Jan. 1960, 43-44

Hays, H. R. "Laforgue and Wallace Stevens," *Romanic Review*, XXV (1934) 242-248.

Heringman, B. "Wallace Stevens: The Use of Poetry," *English Literary History*, XVI (1949) 325-36.

Historical Review of Berks County, XXIV, 4 (Fall 1959) (Wallace Stevens number.)

Kermode, Frank. *Wallace Stevens*, New York 1961 (Grove).

Martz, L. L. "The World of Wallace Stevens," *Focus*, V, London, 1950,

"Wallace Stevens: The World as Meditation," *Yale Review*, XLVII (1958) 517-536.

Morse, S. F. "The Native Element," *Kenyon Review*, XX (1958) 446-465.

Pack, Robert. *Wallace Stevens*, New Brunswick (N.J.) 1958.

Ransom, John Crowe. *The World's Body*, New York, 1938.

Schwartz, Delmore. "Instructed of Much Morality," *Sewanee Review*, LIV (1946) 439-449.

Simons, Hi. "The Comedian as the Letter C," *Southern Review*, V (1940), 453-468.

Simons, Hi. "Wallace Stevens and Mallarme," *Modern Philology*, XLIII (1946) 235-259.

Southworth, J. G. *Some Modern American Poets*, Oxford, 1950.

Stallknecht, N. P. "Absence in Reality: A Study in the Epistemology of the Blue Guitar," *Kenyon Review*, XXI (1959) 545-562.

Symonds, Julian. "A Short View of Wallace Stevens," *Life and Letters Today*, XXVI (1946) 215-224.

Taupin, Rene. *L'Influence du Symbolisme Francais sur La Poesie Americaine*, Paris, 1929 (One of the earliest works to take note of Stevens).

Watts, H .H. "Wallace Stevens and the Rock of Summer," *Kenyon Review*, XIV (1952), 122-140.

Wells, Henry W. *Introduction to Wallace Stevens*, Bloomington (Indiana) 1964.

Williams, William Carlos. *Kora in Hell*, Boston, 1920.

Winters, Yvor. *In Defense of Reason*, New York, 1963.

CHECKLIST

Mores, Samuel French. *Wallace Stevens: A Preliminary Checklist of His Published Writings, 1898-1954*, New Haven (Conn.) 1954.

www.ingramcontent.com/pod-product-compliance
Lightning Source LLC
LaVergne TN
LVHW011732060526
838200LV00051B/3151